Sefer Ikkar Ger Toshav

(*B'Zman HaZeh*)

Laws of Ger Toshav

The Gentile Who Rejects Idolatry

Based on the teachings of

HaRav HaGaon Ahron Soloveichik, ztz'l

Chofetz Chaim, Lubavitcher Rebbe, and more

~~

Compiled and translated by

Rabbi David Katz

With respect and gratitude to Rabbi Zev Leff for his valuable input concerning this work.

Edited and prepared for publication by Miriam Leah Ben-Yaacov

FAQ editorial contribution by Shifra Hendrie

Lexicon editorial contribution by Amnon Goldberg

Editorial contribution by Rabbi Zev Leff & Rabbi Chaim Clorfene

Thanks to Russell Kirk and Jacque Kotze for their many study hours, help in refining the text, and diligence to see the project come to its full fruition.

Published by Create Space in the United States of America

ISBN-13: 978-1548563271

ISBN-10: 1548563277

To contact Rabbi David Katz:

soulmazal@gmail.com / katz@getsoulstrong.com

In Israel: 050-5773-444

From the US: (702) 577-1891

Get Soul Strong online learning of Universal Torah:

https://www.getsoulstrong.com.

Rabbi Katz's other books are available for purchase (online at Amazon.com):

- ***The World of the Ger***
- ***Soul Mazal***

For hardback editions of ***The World of the Ger*** and/or translations of Rabbi Ahron Soloveichik's ***Ode Yisrael Yosef Beni Chai*** [*Siman* 3 concerning *Ger Toshav b'zman hazeh*], contact Russell Kirk at ger@getsoulstrong.com.

Rabbi Zev Leff

Rabbi of Moshav Matityahu

Rosh HaYeshiva—Yeshiva Gedola Matityahu

הרב זאב לף

מרא דאתרא מושב מתתיהו

ראש הישיבה—ישיבה גדולה מתתיהו

D.N. Modiin 71917   Tel: 08—976—1138 טל'   Fax: 08—976—5326 פקס'   ד.נ. מודיעין 71917

Dear Friends,

I have read portions of the "Sefer Ikkar Ger Toshav (B'zman Hazeh)" by Rabbi David Katz. Rabbi Katz elucidates the concept of a Ger Toshav as it applied in the time that yovel was effective and as it applies in a limited fashion even today. His presentation is based primarily on the exposition of his Rebbe, HaRav HaGaon Aharon Soloveitchik zt"l. He also quotes other sources in the Rishonim and Achronim as well as contemporary sources such as the Mishna Brura, Rav Hutner zt"l, and the Lubavitcher Rebbe zt"l.

Rabbi Katz is to be commended for bringing to the attention of the community the often misunderstood distinctions between different classifications of non-jews and the halachos that apply to each specific classification.

Rabbi Katz presents the sources and various opinions regarding the contempory status of a ger toshav. The halachic conclusions derived from this discussion should be decided by one's competent Rav and posek.

I commend Rabbi Katz for an eyeopening, well researched presentation and pray that Hashem bless him with life and health and the wherewithal to continue to merit the community.

Sincerely,
With Torah blessings

Rabbi Zev Leff

RABBI MOSHE MEIR GARFUNKEL
2510 S. GREEN ROAD
UNIVERSITY HTS., OHIO 44122
(216)291-5000

משה מאיר גארפונקקל
רב
ק"ק זכרון חיים
קליוולאנד, אהייא

בס"ד

October 19, 2017

Dear Rabbi David Katz,

Thank you very much for sharing your
Kuntras on geirus. I went through
some of it and am happy to say I gained
much from it. You are to be commended for
putting out a good source of information.

I honestly believe you should be a source
for disseminating these halachos

May Hashem grant you long life and happiness
and success in this and other pursuits.

Sincerely,

6

TABLE OF CONTENTS

Foreword

The Noahide and the Ger Toshav

Ger Toshav is a universally accepted Torah concept that exists today and spans the entire *Mesora*. A Noahide is a follower of the Seven Laws of Noah while a *Ger Toshav* is the distinction given to one who has formally accepted (*kabbalah*) upon one's self the Seven Laws. All *Gerei Toshav* are Noahides, but not all Noahides are *Gerei Toshav*. One must pay special attention to the terminologies; they are not dogmatic, and context will determine meaning.

The Rabbis have established a vernacular for the non-Jew in Torah, and each term may carry several connotations. Careful study is a pre-requisite when studying the non-Jew in Torah. Case in point: a Noahide may imply an adherent to the Seven Laws of Noah, or it can just mean a religious non-Jew. Or a *Ger Toshav* (in text) may refer to a resident alien at a time of Jubilee, or it can mean someone (today) who has rejected idols (properly). Knowing the terminologies and Torah discussions of this subject matter will give deeper understanding to the non-Jew in Torah.

Every sect of Torah Judaism and selected sages of Israel have written about the *Ger Toshav*, and in particular, its relevance today. Torah luminaries, spanning from The Lubavitcher Rebbe,

9

The Chofetz Chaim, Rebbe Nachman, The Gaon of Vilna, Rabbi Ahron Soloveichik, and many more, have written about the *Ger Toshav* that was brought down in *Chazal* and elucidated by the *Rishonim*. As we all know, the sages of Israel have been known to disagree on certain matters. But the *Ger Toshav* has a unanimous standing among all sages; there is universal agreement about the fundamentals of *Ger Toshav*, and its status for today in particular.

We have all been told at one point in time that the *Ger Toshav* does not exist today. The truth of the matter is that this is only half-true. There are some types of *Ger Toshav* that in fact do exist today, i.e. those not connected to the Jubilee Year. However, when one fully looks into the subject matter of *Ger Toshav*, one will soon realize that the writings of the sages are unified and that *Ger Toshav* (non-Jubilee) is a real person as represented through *halacha* for today's Torah world.

One practical example (in *halacha*) is the non-Jew who has <u>accepted</u> the Seven Laws of Noah; he is removed from being a *Shabbos Goy*.[1] The distinction between *Ger Toshav* and Noahide carries heavy consequences; a Noahide remains a Shabbos goy. The distinction [between the two] comes down to whether or not one has fully rejected idolatry (*Shituf*) on the Torah level. This alone can make one a *Ger Toshav* [of today].

---

[1] See footnote 77 on pg 122.

Ger Toshav of today can be best summarized with a verse in *Parashas Re'eh* 14:21: 'Give the *Neveilah* (non-*kosher* meat) to the *Ger in your Gates* or sell it to the *Nochri* (gentile).' This *Mitzvah* (that can even be performed today) demands that one can successfully identify the difference between a *Nochri* and a *Ger Toshav* (in your gates). The *Nochri* is a *'goy/acum'* and the *Ger* (in your gates) is a *Ger Toshav* through a personal acceptance of the Seven Laws of Noah.

This insight is enough to encourage any reader to look further into this subject matter. Even one with marginal interest will see the beauty and unity of the Torah (of the *Ger Toshav*) of Moses as expressed through the generations of the Sages of Israel.

Rabbi David Katz
Modi'in Israel

Statement of Objective

When a Rabbi in Israel writes a responsum to a question dealing with our responsibilities to a non-Jew, all of the background material we have discussed is taken for granted. Without it, one cannot begin to understand what the responsum is all about.

For centuries, we were besieged and beleaguered, hounded and persecuted. Every diabolical stratagem was applied to destroy the spirit and the body of those who remained loyal. And yet we survived – not, as might be expected, embittered and hardened beyond the capacity for humane feeling and compassion. Not so! Our fathers, who suffered in the ghettos of the middle ages and the pale of Russia, and our brothers, who in our own day felt the satanic fury of accursed Nazidom, were not brutalized by the enormity of their suffering.

The more they suffered, the deeper did Jews penetrate to the meaning of the *Halakha* about man and the more truly did their day-to-day practice reflect the highest response to God's imperative. Compassion and mercy for all men are the mark of the Jew, just as they are of God. As Rabbi Akiva said, 'Beloved is man for he was created in the image of God. . . . Beloved is Israel for they are called 'children of God.' '

~Rabbi Nachum Eliezer Rabinovitch~

Our objective is to bring out the *Ger Toshav sugia* for the reasons stated by Rabbi Rabinovitch. Our message is in contrast to the other Noahide organizations whose well-intentioned initiative is to conceal the *Ger Toshav* sugia. The entire Torah of the non-Jew is contained within the *Ger Toshav*[2] *sugia*, the *Ger in your gate* of the *Chumash*.

The main body of this work is comprised of two books: Rabbi Ahron Soloveichik's "*Ode Yisrael Yosef Beni Chai*" and Rabbi Nachum Eliezer Rabinovitch's *halachic* teachings and responsa. Also included are teachings of other rabbinic authorities on *Ger Toshav*, including the Lubavitcher Rebbe, Chofetz Chaim, the Brisker Rav and others, along with an interpretive elucidation as an aide to studying the *Ger Toshav sugia* as it exists today.

---

[2] Rambam *Hilchot Melachim* 8:10-11 and its practical application today for the non-Jews who reject idolatry and wish to serve Hashem the proper way by the standards of *halacha*. See Lubavitcher Rebbe's commentary on the Rambam concerning *Ger Toshav*.

"Rabbi Katz presents the sources and various opinions regarding the contempory status of a *Ger toshav*. The *halachic* conclusions derived from this discussion should be decided by one's competent Rav and posek." - Rabbi Zev Leff

Rabbi Zev Leff

Rabbi of Moshav Matityahu
Rosh HaYeshiva—Yeshiva Gedola Matityahu

בס"ד

הרב זאב לף

מרא דאתרא מושב מתתיהו
ראש הישיבה—ישיבה גדולה מתתיהו

D.N. Modiin 71917   Tel: 08—976—1138 טל׳   Fax: 08—976—5326 פקס׳   ד.נ. מודיעין 71917

Dear Friends,

I have read Rabbi David Katz's translation of the Third Chapter of the book "Od Yisroel Yosef B'ni Chai" by HaRav Aaron Soloveichek zatzal. The chapter deals with the issue of visiting non Jewish people who are sick to avoid animosity. The presentation is an involved and intricate halachic discourse. The presentation also defines the various designations of non-Jew including the designation of the "Ger Toshav".

Rabbi David Katz has faithfully translated this chapter and has thus provided a benefit to those who cannot follow the discussion in the original Hebrew. The discussion itself is an eye-opener as the various designations of non-Jew and the laws pertinent to them are often not known or distorted.

I commend Rabbi Katz for his effort and pray that Hashem grant him life, health and the wherewithal to continue to merit the community with further works.

Sincerely,

With Torah blessings

Zev Leff

Rabbi Zev Leff

17

Congregation Beth Sholom Ahavas Achim
5665 North Jersey Avenue
Chicago, IL 60659

1/8/17

Rabbi David Katz has dedicated his life to the study of Torah and has taken a special interest in the study of halachas regarding the relationship between Jew and non-Jew. He has organized a group who share this interest with him. Rabbi Katz has compiled divrei halachah of the Gedolai Yisroel (leading Torah scholars throughout the generations) who have written on this halachic topic.

It is unfortunate that much of the attitudes of our community concerning this subject was and is acquired only through osmosis of the historical experiences of our community rather than through the actual study of the texts of the oral tradition. To help rectify this situation, Rabbi Katz has spearheaded a drive to study our sacred text on this subject. He has taken the Torah thoughts of our great Rabbis and translated them in English, which could serve as an aid in studying the original texts. Among the texts translated, is a section from the book written by my father ZT"L (dealing with the laws of visiting the sick and the laws of mourning). This collection is not being made for sale or profit, but only as an aid for those involved in the group who are focused on the study of the halachas.

While I have not the time to thoroughly look over the translation of the essay written by my father ZT"L, having studied the original composed with my father's clarity and depth it is my feeling that making the study of these texts available to even those who otherwise would not be able to acquire a true understanding of these topics will help, not only in promoting Torah learning on a higher level, but will contribute to alleviating the misconception that many have concerning the halachah (Jewish law) about relationships between Jew and non-Jew.

May this endeavor be successful in promoting peace among mankind and fulfillment of the mitzvah of following in the path of G-d in the showing of mercy to all those created in His image.

sincerely yours,

Rabbi Moshe Soloveichik

Excerpts and Elucidations from

Rabbi Ahron Soloveichik's

Ode Yisrael Yosef Beni Chai

~~

The following is an adaptation of Rabbi David Katz's translation of

Rabbi Ahron Soloveichik's

'*Ode Yisrael Yosef Beni Chai*'

1) The *goyim* in our times are generally categorized in Torah as, [we are to] 'help them and do not hurt them.' This obligates us to save them and give them sustenance. And they have the status of a *Ger Toshav* in some respects, but they are not complete *Gerei Toshav,* which exists only in times when the Jubilee Year is operative, when they are to accept upon themselves (*kabbalah*) their Noahide obligation before three Israelites which *Ha-Kodesh Baruch Hu* commanded in the Torah as explained by the Rambam in *Hilchot Melachim chapter 8.*

2) This matter is explained through *Meiri* in *Avodah Zara 26,*[3] where he writes: 'in our times they acknowledge the Creator of the world' and the *Tzemach Tzedek, Hilchot Ribit,* writes that the *goyim* in our times acknowledge the Creator of the Universe. They have the (status) of a *Ger Toshav* as long as they do not violate other transgressions of the Seven Laws of Noah, and we have a *mitzvah* to support them.

3) The *Arukh Ha-Shulchan, Yoreh Deah 254*, paragraph 3, writes that in general we have a *mitzvah* to help

---

[3] As well as many other places: *Bava Kamma 38, and Yoma, and Ketubot 16,* and look in the *Be'er HaGolah in Yoreh Deah 266.*

provide the *goyim* in our times with a livelihood, as with the *Ger Toshav* in the days of the Holy Temple.

4) The *Shailat Yavetz 41* writes that even according to the view that *B'nai Noah* are warned against *shituf* (attributing partnership with God; the Rambam's view). Nevertheless, the *goyim* in our times are categorized as, 'help them and do not hurt them,' because the *halacha* of *acum* (*goyim*) that live outside of the Land of Israel is that they are not considered idol worshippers. Rather they are merely following the practices of their forefathers. This is similar to serving idols under duress or by coercion.

5) The *acum* that live outside the land of Israel, are raised as idolaters. If they are not transgressors of the other transgressions of the *Seven Mitzvot B'nai Noah*, and they function as idolaters only because of the customs of their forefathers, then they have the status of being *anusin* (coerced) and the Torah prohibition of 'do not be gracious to them,' does not apply to them. Look in the *Radvaz* in his responsa, Section 4, number 526, where he writes, 'according to the position of Rabbenu Tam who says that *B'nai Noah* are not prohibited from *shituf*, therefore, the prohibition of 'you shall not be gracious to them' is not applicable to *Notzrim*.'

6) And even according to the opinion that *shituf* is forbidden to *B'nai Noah* (the *Rambam's* opinion), in any case, since the *nochrim* who are outside the land of Israel are not fully idolaters, but rather follow the customs of their forefathers, automatically the prohibition of 'do not be gracious to them,' is not relevant to them.

7) It is explained in the words of the *Radak* that a *nochri*, even though he may transgress any or all of the *Seven Mitzvot B'nai Noah*, if he acts with kindness towards Israel, and even if he is *acum* living in the land of Israel not under coercion, then not only are we allowed to do good to him, we are obligated to do good to him.

8) The *halacha* that the *Radak* mentions is in agreement with the *Gemara* in *Megillah 6a*. And look in *Sefer Chassidim* where it is written that if there is a particular *acum* who acts with kindness towards Israel, if he is sick, we are obligated to pray on his behalf, and when he dies we are to say *zichrona l'bracha* (may he remembered for a blessing).

9) In relation to the *acum*, there is a prohibition against being gracious to him, for one may not compliment him, even to say: 'how handsome this *acum* is,' unless he has in mind to praise *Hashem*. And definitely,

saying 'zichrona l'bracha' is the highest praise in the world. So how can we possibly praise *acum* who generally transgress the *Seven Mitzvot B'nai Noah*? Rather, it is certain that the prohibition against being gracious to the *acum* is predicated on the *acum* being considered as completely wicked. And if he does good for Israel, then he does not carry the stigma of being considered as completely wicked.

10) The Rambam, *Hilchot Melachim 10:10* writes, 'If a *Ben Noah* wants to do a *mitzvah* from the other *mitzvot* of the Torah in order to receive reward, we don't prevent him if he does it according to *halacha*, and if he brings a burnt-offering (*korban olah*), we accept it from him. And if he gives *tzedaka*, we accept it from him. And it appears that we may give it [his *tzedaka*] to the poor of Israel, since he is sustained by Israel, and Israel is commanded to support him. If an *acum* gives charity, we may take it from him, but we give it to the *acum* poor.' However, we can receive charity from a *Ben Noah,* and it is not forbidden, since we are also commanded to give them charity because of lovingkindness and not just because of *darchei shalom*[4] alone. This is even if he is not a *Ger Toshav*

---

[4] peaceful relations.

Gamor,[5] who has properly accepted upon himself in front of the *bet din* the *Seven Mitzvot B'nai Noah* in a time when the Jubilee Year is operative. It is permissible because *Hashem* commanded it in the Torah by the hand of Moshe Rabbeinu, and therefore the Rambam in this *halacha* does not use the term *Ger Toshav*, but rather expresses it as *Ben Noah*.

11) A *nochri,* who does not usually transgress the *Seven Laws of B'nai Noah*, has the *din* of 'help him and do not hurt him,' and we are commanded to support him.

12) The *Radvaz* and *Shailat Yavetz* add to this that even *nochrim,* who are truly *acum,* but do not serve idols with conscious intent, rather they follow a custom inherited from their forefathers, also are categorically designated as 'help them and do not hurt them,' because the prohibition of 'do not be gracious to them' concerns only the '*wicked* among the *acum.*' These are *acum* who were in Israel in the time of the Temple when Israel had the upper hand.

13) I wrote above, concerning that which was written by HaRav HaMeiri, that in many places in *Shaas, Baba Kama, Avodah Zara, Ketubot, and Yoma,* that, in general, the Gentiles of our times are bound by their

---

[5] a complete *Ger Toshav.*

religious perspective; they have the *din* of a *Ger Toshav* of the time of the Temple, and consequently, we are commanded to support them, and it is forbidden to take their lost possessions just as it is forbidden to take the lost items of an Israelite. And this matter is stated in the same way by the *Be'er Ha-Golah in Choshen Mishpat* 425 and 266. And also, the *Tzemach Tzedek* in *Yoreh Deah, Hilchot Ribit,* says this.

14) The *Arukh Ha-Shulchan* in *Yoreh Deah, Hilchot Tzedakah 254,* rules that the Gentiles of our times have the *din* of a *Ger Toshav,* and we are commanded to support them. Also, Rav Tzvi Hirsch Chayot, in his work *Tiferet Yisrael,* rules according to *halacha* that the Gentiles of our period have the *din* of a *Ger Toshav,* because the *B'nai Noah* are not forbidden to believe in *shituf.*[6] Also, the *Gra* on *Orukh Chaim* 159 ruled like *Rabbeinu Tam* that *B'nai Noah* are not forbidden *shituf.* The Gaon Rabbi Eliyahu Henkin, *z'l,* wrote that the Gentiles of our times have the *din* of *Ger Toshav,* and we are obligated to support them and save them from all danger and difficulty. But since we do not fully accept *Ger Toshav,* except in the times when the Jubilee Year is operative, therefore, we are not obligated to provide them with sustenance to the

---

[6] partnership with Hashem.

same extent as with an Israelite, according to the principle of: 'We are to give him what he no longer possesses.'

15) The *Griz, ztz'l,* in his *sefer,* explains the verse 'do not deliver a slave to his master, that he should be safe with you away from the nation of his master. With you he shall dwell in your midst in a place that he will choose in one of your cities that is good for him; do not taunt him.'

From this, we can rule in two matters:

a) a Canaanite slave who flees from a land outside Israel to the land of Israel;

b) and concerning a *Ger Toshav,* who comes to settle in the land of Israel in the time that the Jubilee Year is observed.

For with respect to both of these categories, the Torah says, '*He shall dwell with you in your midst and it should go well with him; do not taunt him.*'[7] The *Sifri* comments on this verse, where it says, '*with you he shall dwell,*' in the city itself, and not by the border, '*in a place that he will choose,*' in a place where he will be able to find a livelihood, in one of your cities so that he should not wander from city

---

[7] *Devarim* 23:17.

to city; '*it should be good for him,*' from a bad dwelling to a nice dwelling.

16) The command concerning a *Ben Noah*, who properly accepts upon himself the *Seven Mitzvot B'nai Noah* before three (Men of Israel) in a time when the Jubilee is observed, is that we make him equal to Israel in the *mitzvah* of charity, to make it possible for him to attain his livelihood in a good way. That is to say, that we are commanded to provide as his livelihood, not merely a meager subsistence, but a generous income, consistent with the principle of, 'It is sufficient to provide him with whatever he is lacking.'

17) Based on *Rashi* in *Arachin* 29, it is implied from the text that 'there is no *Ger Toshav* observed except in a time when Jubilee is observed,' and the Torah's mandate to equate the *Ger Toshav* with the Israelite is only in a time when the Jubilee Year is observed. But in a time when the Jubilee Year is not operative, we are not commanded to make him equal to Israel.

18) In relation to the *mitzvah* of 'And you will strengthen [your brother] - *Ger* and *Toshav* -and he will he will live with you.'[8] There is a mandate according to the *Ramban* that 'we are commanded to vitalize '*Ger* and

---

[8] *Vayikra 25:35.*

Toshav' to save him from his troubles. This means if he is drowning in a river, or if enough rubbish crashes upon him that requires all our strength to rescue him, or if he is sick, we have to tend to his healing.'[9]

19) This *mitzvah* is operative even when the Jubilee Year is not operative, and even if he has not accepted upon himself before three Israelites to keep the Seven *Mitzvot*; it is enough for us to know that he does not transgress them. Then we are obligated to rescue him from all trouble and danger. But the *mitzvah* of 'with you he shall dwell in your midst and it shall be good for him; do not taunt him,'[10] is not relevant except for a *Ger Toshav* at a time when the Jubilee Year is observed.

20) The *chidushim* of Rabbenu Yonah on *Sanhedrin* 57, explicitly writes that a *Ben Noah* who keeps *Seven Mitzvot B'nai Noah*, [even though he did not accept them upon himself in front of three Israelites], obligates us to rescue him from danger. And look in *Sefer Yeraim* 233, where it is written, if a *goy* keeps the Seven *Mitzvot*, we must count him as a *Ger Toshav*, and we are commanded to support him even in a time when the Jubilee Year is not observed.

---

[9] *Ramban* in *Sefer HaMitzvos* Positive *Mitzvah* #16.
[10] *Devarim* 23:17.

21) The *Ravad* on *Hilchot Assurei Biah 14:8*, wrote that there is a <u>distinction</u> of *Ger Toshav* even when the Jubilee Year is not operative. But with regard to the obligation to support him broadly, with the same degree of support as an Israelite, we are not obligated to do so when the Jubilee Year is not operative, because it is the Jubilee Year which mandates this. In times when the Jubilee Year is operative, they observe *shmitta,* and they are able to provide support without making it a burden on the community, which is not the case now. It appears that the *Ravad*, holds like *Rashi* on *Arachin 29a,* that the *halacha* of 'Ger Toshav only occurs at a time when the Jubilee Year is observed,' is only relevant with respect to the scriptural command, '*with you he will live in your midst and it will be good for him,*' and this obligation exists only when we observe Jubilee.

22) However, the view of the Rambam is not so. And it was explained by my uncle, the *Griz*, at the end of his book, look there at what he wrote: 'that the entire <u>distinction</u> of *Ger Toshav* is based only on his right to live in the land of Israel, and is not relevant to the *Ger Toshav* himself, for he does not accomplish anything new through his personal acceptance [of the Seven Laws of Noah].

And his essential being as a *Ger Toshav* is only to attach to Israel in order to dwell in the land of Israel, and concerning this do we have the stipulation of 'there is no *Ger Toshav* except in a time when the Jubilee Year is operative.' About this, I wondered that surely there are many *statutes* that have nothing to do with dwelling in the land of Israel, and they are explicitly applicable to the *Ger Toshav* and not the *Ben Noah*. For example, a *Ben Noah* is killed over manslaughter, while a *Ger Toshav*, who kills inadvertently, is punished with exile. And there are many other examples. Behold, the *kabbalah*/personal acceptance made by the *Ger Toshav* carries with it new statutes, also to the *Ger Toshav* himself. The Torah itself makes a clear distinction between a *Ger Toshav* and a *Ben Noah*... According to this, then it is fair to say that the *din* is that there is no *Ger Toshav* except in a time of the Jubilee Year. According to the thinking of the Rambam, the essence of the *distinction* is that in a time when there is no Jubilee Year, there is no *din* of *Ger Toshav,* and this results in his being no different from a regular *Ben Noah*. And look in the *Maggid Mishneh* on the laws of *Issurei Biah* (Forbidden Relationships), who wrote that this is also the simple explanation of the view of the Rambam. However, the *Ravad* has a different view of the matter. He holds that only with respect (to a few) specific laws does the distinction of the *Ger Toshav* depend on its observance of the Jubilee Year. But the view of the Rambam seems simple and clear.' The *Griz* explains that according to the *shittat ha*-Rambam, 'there is no *din* of a *Ger Toshav* at all in a time when the Jubilee Year is not observed.'

23) *HaRav HaMeiri* writes in several places of the Talmud, that the nations which follow the ways of religion and doctrine carry the <u>distinction</u> of *Ger Toshav*, and we are obligated to support them.

24) And look in *Sefer V'Shav HaKohen* of the *gaon* Rafael Hamburg, *z'l*, who wrote that even according to the view of Rebbeinu Tam and the Rabbeinu Yonah, *B'nai Noah* are not forbidden *shituf.* Nevertheless, the *Ger Toshav is forbidden shituf.*

25) It appears that according to the Rambam, there are two types of *Ger Toshav*:

   a) A *Ger Toshav Gamor* who accepts upon himself Seven *Mitzvot B'nai Noah*, since they were commanded to Israel at Mara.

   b) A *Ger Toshav* who keeps Seven *Mitzvot* since they were commanded to Adam and Noah.

And this second type of *Ger Toshav* does not fall into the name or category of '*Ger Toshav*,' because he did not accept them <u>before a *bet din* Yisrael</u>. However, we are commanded to support him, because he is permitted to dwell in the land of Israel.

And look in the Rambam, *Issurei Biah 14:7*, where he writes: 'Who is a *Ger Toshav*? He is an *acum*, who accepts upon himself not to serve idols with the rest of the *mitzvot* that were commanded to *B'nai Noah*, and he has not been circumcised nor has he immersed in a *mikvah*. Behold, we accept him, and he is considered from the *Chasidei Umot HaOlam* (Pious ones from the nations of the world). Why do we call his name '*Toshav*'? It is because we are permitted to settle him among us in the land of Israel just like it we explained in *Hilchot Acum*.'

And in *halacha* 8 it is written: 'And we do not proactively receive the *Ger Toshav* except in a time when the Jubilee Year is observed. But in our times, even if he accepts upon himself the entire Torah, with the exception of one minute detail, we do not proactively receive him.' These are the words of the Rambam.

And it follows that even in the time when the Jubilee is not observed, he is considered a *Ger Toshav,* and we are commanded to support him. And in *halacha* 8, the Rambam writes, 'But we do not accept a *Ger Toshav* [in *bet din*] except when the Jubilee is observed, thus when the Jubilee in not observed, we do not accept him [in *bet din*].' This means that when the Jubilee is not observed, even if he is careful to observe the Seven *Mitzvot,* he does not have the <u>distinction</u> of a full *Ger Toshav,* and we are not obligated to support him in the same way as either a *Ger Toshav* without *bet din*, or in a time when the Jubilee is not observed.

26) Behold we see from *Sefer Yeraim* that the prohibition of 'do not settle them' applies only to those who transgress the *Seven Mitzvot B'nai Noah,* but not to a *goy* who does not transgress, even though he did not accept [the Seven Laws] upon himself, in *bet din,* at a time of Jubilee.

27) A *Ben Noah* is a *goy* who does not accept upon himself the Seven *Mitzvot* in front of a *bet din* of Israelites; rather, he is a Gentile, whom we have established as one who does not transgress the Seven *Mitzvot.* Although he is not called a *Ger Toshav Gamor;* still, he is included in the *mitzvah* of, '*Ger and Toshav he should*

live with you,' and we are obligated only to save him from trials and hardships, and, therefore, we are permitted to give their *tzedaka* to the poor of Israel. The Rambam in *Hilchot Zichiya u'Matanah*, says that it is allowed to give a free gift to every *Ger Toshav* who does not transgress *Seven Mitzvot B'nai Noah*, citing the verse, '*Ger* and *Toshav* and he shall live with you.'

28) *HaRav HaMeiri* on *Avodah Zara* 26 writes these words: 'the *goyim* and shepherds of flocks [sheep and goats] of Israelites are blocked from providing sacrifices because of the suspicion of robbery and depravity, indicating that they threw off the yoke of Torah; they do this not because they lack being religious, but because of money [and lust]. Nevertheless, whatever troubles come to them are their own fault and we are not obligated to help them or save them.'

29) And besides this, with *goyim*, one needs to investigate their prior actions before dealing with a specific *goy*. That is to say, with idol worshippers, whom we would not consider as having religion and tradition. (The typical idol worshipper, in the times of *Chazal* were sunken into sinning and crookedness, such as robbery and sexual sins, and were suspected of murdering

34

Jews, and it was forbidden to make any connection with them.)

30) And it is obvious from the language of *HaRav HaMeiri* that only idol worshippers who view every transgression and crooked behavior as good in their eyes are excluded from being saved by us and are in the category of: 'do not help them and do not hurt them.' If they are sullied by transgression and crookedness, then the <u>distinction</u>, 'do not help them and do not hurt them,' applies. And the position of *Tosefot* in *Chullin* 13, is that the <u>distinction</u> of, 'do not help them and do not hurt them,' is relevant only to *acum* in *Eretz Yisrael* who were not under duress [from their parents and environment], and it is as written by *Shiurei Karbon* in *Gittin* who argues on the language of the Rambam in *Hilchot Melachim* with respect to the *acum* outside the land of Israel who <u>are</u> under duress, then we are obligated to save them from every trouble because of mercy, as in, '*Hashem is good to all and His mercy is above all his deeds.*'

31) Therefore, our sages say that the *Chasidei Umot HaOlam* have a share of the World to Come if they comprehend what is fitting to comprehend of the knowledge of the blessed Creator, and they refine their souls by rectifying their character traits. And

there is no doubt that anyone who refines himself with proper character traits and proper wisdom, with faith in the blessed Creator, has a portion of the World to Come. And therefore, our sages, the sages of true wisdom, have said that even an *acum* who strives in the Torah, behold, he is like a *Kohen Gadol* (a Jewish High Priest).' These are the words of the Rambam.

Summary and Conclusion

~~

by Rabbi David Katz

Today's Torah observant world largely lacks an understanding of the *Ger Toshav*. The current views are formed entirely through 'communal osmosis' and not by the Torah scholarship that it requires.

The *Ger Toshav* does exist today, even according to the Rambam. Today's *Ger Toshav*, however, is not a complete *Ger Toshav*; rather, he has the *din* of *Ger Toshav* in selected matters.

The Ten Commandments commands us to rest the *Ger in your Gates*. The sages learn from this that one who is not the *Ger in your Gates* is a *nochri* and can be used as a 'Shabbos goy.' We learn from this that the *Ger in your Gates* has a connection to *dinei Yisrael and Torat Yisrael*[11] (laws and teachings that apply to a Jew) and he has a unique commandment concerning his observance of Shabbos, as it says explicitly in *Keritot* 9a. He is the *Ger Toshav* of today.

The *Ger in your Gates* of today seeks to reject (or already has rejected) *shituf* and to live his/her life with an active *belief* in the God of Israel. This is the non-Jew that Rashi's commentary to the first verse of the *Shema*[12] speaks of so highly: '*The Lord who is our God now, and not the God of the other nations, will be in the*

---

[11] *Litukei Sichos* Vol 31, *Parashas Mishpatim.*

[12] *Devarim* 6:4.

future One Lord, as it is stated,[13] *'for then I will turn to the peoples a pure language, that they may all call upon the Name of the Lord, and it is stated,*[14] *'In that day shall the Lord be One and His Name One.'*

Rashi's future is our present. And it is every Torah observant Jew's obligation to make a profound paradigm shift; to go from learning this matter by osmosis, to pursuing it from the truth of the Torah.

---

[13] *Zeph. 3:9.*

[14] *Zech.14:9.*

Rabbi Nachum Eliezer Rabinovitch

The following is Rabbi David Katz's unofficial translation and compilation of Rabbi Rabinovitch's *halachic* works concerning *Ger Toshav*, including unofficial translation of **SHU'T Siach Nachum #93** concerning *Ger Toshav b'zman hazeh.*

A *Ger* [*Chasid*] *Toshav* who wants to settle in The Land of Israel amidst The Nation of Israel, and properly accepts [*kabbalah*] upon himself [as such] before three [Jewish] men[15]...if he wants to gird himself with additional *Mitzvot* beyond the Seven Laws of Noah, behold, this is not considered 'making a new religion.' For a *Ger Toshav* [which cannot be a *Yovel Ger Toshav*, for Rambam *Hilchot Melachim* 8:10-11 is not speaking about a *Ger Toshav*, see *Siach Nachum* 93] is not prohibited from Studying Torah or from Keeping Shabbos, that behold, it is not his desire to create a new religion nor to enlist innocent Jews into a new religion.

Commentary to *Sefer Shoftim*: Rabbi Nachum Eliezer Rabinovitch in reference to *Hilchot Melachim* 10:9

---

[15] Rambam *Hilchot Melachim* 8:10-11

SHU"T Siach Nachum

Rabbi Nachum Eliezer Rabinovitch

93. Ger Toshav of Today

Question:

What is the opinion of the Rav about the proper treatment of individuals from the *Umot HaOlam* (Nations of the World) who are [currently] peaceful with us? Is there [the *din* of] *'Ger Toshav'* today?

Answer:

In the complex matter of *Ger Toshav*, look at what I wrote about this in relation to medical treatment for *Nochri* on Shabbos in [my] *Shaylot* and *Teshuvot 'M'Lumdei Milchama'*.[16] Whereas the words of the Rambam stand to support him in this complex matter of the categorical *Ger Toshav* of our time, we will discuss below his opinion.

---

[16] *Siman* 43.

א. Distinguishing between the terms *'Ger Toshav'* and *'Chasid Umot HaOlam'*

The Rambam wrote:[17] *'Adam HaRishon* was commanded on six things:

1) *Avodah Zara*
2) Birkas Hashem
3) Murder
4) Immorality
5) Stealing
6) *Dinim*

To Noah was added, 'eating the limb of a living animal,' as it says, 'Thus the flesh with its soul in its blood, you shall not eat';[18] it turns out that there are seven commandments.' There above[19] Rabbeinu established: 'All who accept the Seven Commandments, and are careful to keep them – behold, this [shows that one is] **'From the Chasidei Umot HaOlam'** and dually has a portion of the World to Come.' However, before this, he established:[20] 'And the one that accepts them – is called *Ger Toshav* in

---

[17] *Hilchot Melachim 9:1.*

[18] *Breshit 9:4.*

[19] *Hilchot Melachim 8:11.*

[20] *Hilchot Melachim 8:10.*

every place, and needs to accept them upon one's self before three men.'

Are the concepts **Ger Toshav and Chasid...**the same, or is there a difference between them? And if so, what is the difference between them? The matter comes out clear from the continuation of his words concerning *Chasidei...*, and this is what he said:[21] Behold, this [is from] the *Chasidei...*and he who accepts them and is careful to perform them as Hashem commanded in the Torah as made known through Moshe Rabbeinu [the same as] the *B'nai Noah* were originally commanded in them. But if they perform them from self-determination – this is not *Ger Toshav*, nor are they [from the] *Chasidei...*, rather they are from their 'intellectuals.' Behold, there are clearly three types/terms:

1) *Ger Toshav*
2) *Chasid Umot HaOlam*
3) Intellectuals from the Nations of the World

Ostensibly it would have occurred to us that perhaps *Ger Toshav* is one who has accepted upon himself the commandments alone, but still has not performed them, and when he actually performs them he merits the level 'Chasid...,' that behold, the *Chasid* is categorized as such:

---

[21] *Hilchot Melachim* 8:11.

43

'All who **accept** the Seven Laws and are careful **to do them** in contrast to *Ger Toshav*, there [by *Ger Toshav*] it mentions only **'the one who accepts them.'** However, if this is so, it is possible that if he merely performed them [based off of] intellectually, would his *kabbalah*[22] before three men be nullified; would he be a *Ger Toshav*? And it should be considered that after he took *kabbalah* before three men according to Jewish Faith and Torah Law and was made *Ger Toshav*, would that nullify his giur since he did not have a proper *kavannah* at the time of fulfilling his commandments? On this I wondered!

Clearly therefore, the distinction between *Ger Toshav* and *Chasid*...needs an explanation. In addition to this, there is another problem. In many places Rabbeinu established: 'We do not accept (*mekablin*) *Ger Toshav* except in a time of *Yovel Noheg*, but when it is not a time of *Yovel*, we only accept *Ger Tzedek* alone.' It appears in the continuation that there are basically many contradictions in this *halacha*. In the midst of clarifying and settling these contradictions, one will reach a full category of *Ger Toshav*, which will also solve the first problem, which is to distinguish between *Ger Toshav* and *Chasid*...

---

[22] personal acceptance.

ב. Is there a *Ger Toshav* Today?

First, we need to discuss the contradictions that determine [the conditions of the precept]: 'not to accept *Ger Toshav* today.'

By offering the *din* of '*Ger Tzedek* who regrets this,' Rabbeinu ruled in *Hilchot Melachim* (10:3) as such: 'a *Ben Noah* who is *Nisgaire* and is circumcised and has gone to the *mikvah*, and afterward wants to renege on going in the way of God and to be *Ger Toshav* alone, as he was before, we are not to listen to him. And if he was a child when he went to the *mikvah* through *Bet din* then he is able to renege at the time of his maturity, **and be *Ger Toshav* alone**. And since he did not renege at that time, he may no longer protest; rather he is a *Ger Tzedek*.'

Ger Tzedek who regrets this

The first part of this *halacha* is basically without understanding. If it is speaking about a unique situation of a *Ben Noah* who was first made a *Ger Toshav* and afterward he was made into a *Ger Tzedek*, and therefore he possibly wants to return to being a *Ger Toshav* alone, **as he was before**? If so, behold, the *din* is not possible unless it is a time of *Yovel Noheg*; how did we not feel this limitation? And how is the continuation, in regard to a child that received *mikvah* from the *Bet din*, and it wasn't explained that there is a fundamental and essential difference in the *din* based on when there is a time that is *Yovel Noheg* and today? However, if we say that these matters are as they are simply stated, that this *halacha* is also appropriate for today, surely this will produce a '*Chiddush Gadol*' that it is possible that at first, he was a *Ger Toshav,* and in the end he was a *Ger Tzedek*, and how could this be?

However, the end part of this *halacha* also offers a possibility of how there is also a *Ger Toshav* today. A youth who converts through *Bet din* and grows up only to renege, – he **is a *Ger Toshav* alone**. This *din* also needs an explanation. How is this possible today? Also, one must consider that per force there is no *kabbalah* at play, for he was a child, and thus no *kabbalah* could be considered as *kabbalah*, and in his maturity, it does not mention that he needs any *kabbalah* at all. On the other hand, there is no reason to assume that the first part of the *halacha* speaks about the same scenario as the last part, which is to explain the case as such: a youth who received a *mikvah* through *Bet din* and reneged when he reached maturity and was consequently made a *Ger Toshav*, and later decided to convert, and after that regretted it and wanted to return to be a *Ger Toshav*. If this is the appropriate explanation, then we need to consider the *din* of the last part of the *halacha* first and only after that continue with the *din* of the first part. But the order in which things appear proves that we are speaking of two unique things, which is to say that there are two possibilities that there would be a *Ger Toshav* today.

Eved Canaani **and** Ger Toshav

There is also a third way, and it is even more interesting, from a historical standpoint.

In the days of the Rambam there were still Canaanite Slaves, and in the *Tshuvot* of the *Gaonim* there are many rulings about interacting with slaves like these. Fundamentally, one who acquires an *Eved Canaani* – needs to circumcise him, and through this he enters slightly into *Kedushat Yisrael*, and is obligated in certain clear commandments. But there is a slave who refuses circumcision – what is his *din*? This is explained in *Hilchot Avadim* (8:12):

> One who purchases an *Eved Canaani* from a *stam goy.* and he doesn't want to circumcise or to accept the commandments appropriated for slaves, you are to keep with him for twelve months. If he still doesn't want to do these after the allotted timeframe, then you are to sell him to a *goy* or send him out of The Land. If you stipulated with the slave beforehand that he would not circumcise, behold it is allowed to keep him all the time that he stands fundamentally as a complete *goy*, or you can sell him to *goyim* or send him out of The Land.

Is this *halacha* practical [for today]? Since Rabbeinu didn't indicate otherwise, it appears that this *din* is constant, after all. However, there is a difficulty: 'If the slave stipulated at first that he would not circumcise, behold, it is allowed to keep him **all the**

time he wants as he stands as a complete *goy.*'
What does it mean 'as he stands as a complete *goy*'?
Is the *kavannah* that he retains his idolatrous ways?
And is it allowed for a Jew to keep him in his home if
he is an idolater [practicing idolatry]?

Basically, what is missing here is an explanation from
Hilchot Mila (1:6):

> One who takes a grown slave from the
> *goyim* and he doesn't want to
> circumcise – stay with him for twelve
> months. Any longer, and it is forbidden
> to keep him, as he stands
> uncircumcised; rather he should sell
> him to *goyim*. And if he stipulates this
> at first, and he stands by his master as
> a *goy*, in that he still does not have
> circumcision, it is allowed to keep him
> as he stands uncircumcised, **and only**
> **that he accepts upon himself**
> **(***kabbalah***) the Seven Laws, and he**
> **will be** <u>like</u> **a *Ger Toshav*...** and we
> don't accept (*mekablin*) *Ger Toshav*
> accept in a time of *Yovel Noheg*.

If it says in *Hilchot Avadim* as it says in *Hilchot Mila*, and what isn't explained there is explained here, and in *Hilchot Avadim* we can rely on what was written in *Hilchot Mila* that behold, they appeared earlier? If so, it turns out that the slave stipulated first that he would refuse circumcision, in which case, it is allowed to keep him, but only if he accepted the Seven Laws. Basically, it seems that this *din* is only possible in a time of *Yovel Noheg*, and thus this is how the *halacha* in *Hilchot Mila* ends. But if this is so, this only raises more questions. In *Hilchot Avadim*, which is the *ikkar* of this *halacha*, there isn't even a hint that this *din* is only applicable in a time of *Yovel*, and there it is implied from the mysterious language that this *din* stands forever. However, there is a huge misconception from this; was this *halacha* in its details practical in the days of Rabbeinu?

However, one can see that that there are further details in his language of these *halachot*. If we assume that these two *halachot* are the exact same, it turns out that what was written in *Hilchot Avadim*: 'it is allowed to keep him…as he stands **as a complete goy**' is parallel to what is said in *Hilchot Mila*: 'it is allowed to keep him...and only if he accepts the Seven Laws **and will be like a *Ger Toshav*.'** If it is understood that also a *Ger Toshav* is called a *goy*, then basically this would lower the matter to what was explained in *Hilchot Yayin Nesach* (*Hilchot M'Achlos Assuros* 11:8): 'In every place it says '*stam goy*' behold, this is an idolater.'

The solution to these difficulties reveals with comparison the accepted *halacha* in *Issurei Biah* (14:9):

> A slave taken from the *goyim*, we do not say to him: 'Why did you come?' This we say to them: 'It is your desire into the category of a slave of Israel, and are you of the *kosher* ones, or not?' If he desires, you will let him know of the fundamentals of faith, and give him a *mikvah* to become like a *Ger*.

> And if he does not want to accept, then stay with him for twelve months and sell him to *goyim*, for it is forbidden to keep him more than this. And if he

stipulated with him first to not circumcise or take a *mikvah*, rather to be <u>like</u> a *Ger Toshav* – **you are allowed to keep him in his servitude when he is *Ger Toshav*, and we don't keep a slave like this, except in a time of Yovel.**

This proves that the *din* that is said in *Hilchot Issurei Biah* isn't the same as the *din* said in *Hilchot Avadim*.

In *Hilchot Issurei Biah* it is speaking about a *goy* who is the son of free people, as it came from his own desire and will to sell himself to Israel. But a slave taken from *goyim* – is explained as a slave taken from the *goyim*, and not that his master is a *goy* who sold him. It is in this last point that I wondered more about the language in *Hilchot Avadim* – 'One who purchases a slave from the *goy*.' In *Hilchot Issurei Biah* is explained as: 'We do not say to him – why did you come?' – If it was speaking about a slave purchased from a *goy* [as his master], how will it occur to you to ask him a strange question like this, since by himself he came? Surely his master sold him! Rather, it is clear that the *din* in *Hilchot Issurei Biah* is endorsed on the *goy* who sold himself, and who conditioned upon himself that he is obligated in the Seven Laws, and not like slaves of Israel who are obligated in many more commandments.

This *din* is a straight continuation from what was said in the preceding *halacha* about a regular *Ger Toshav*. First Rabbeinu brought the *din* of a *goy* who is the son of free people who wanted to be a *Ger Toshav* – he is from completely free people, and after that the *din* is of a *goy* who wants to be a *Ger Toshav* who is subordinate to Israel. On this he concludes: That we don't keep a slave like this except in a time of *Yovel*, just like we don't accept (*mekablin*) today a *Ger Toshav* who wants to stay free, thus we don't accept *Ger Toshav* even if he wants to be a slave.

However, as mentioned in *Hilchot Avadim,* he writes explicitly: 'One who purchases a slave.' This slave has no free will, and not by himself did he come to Israel; his master, a *goy*, sold him to Israel against the will of the slave. Rather that in this, the *din* of the slave is that he is able to stipulate at the time of his sale that he forego his circumcision, and 'if he, the slave, stipulated first that he should not circumcise, behold, it is allowed to keep him. However, the Torah maintains that also, if you purchase a Jewish slave from the *goy*, you may not retain him in a Jewish household if he practices idolatry; therefore, the slave needs to accept upon himself the Seven Laws.

But in *Hilchot Mila* we find two situations. Therefore, it begins with the language that can explain both of them – if one takes a grown slave **from the *goyim***, this is said of the slave himself – he who is from the *goyim*, and it is possible that he sold himself or his master, a *goy*, sold him.

And it returns to write that the *din* is accustomed only when he is bought from his master, a *goy,* alone. And it is explicitly saying this: 'And if he conditioned upon himself at first, **and he was by his master, a goy**...it is allowed to keep him...**and only if he accepts upon himself Seven Laws and he will be <u>like</u> a *Ger Toshav*.**' This condition helps only if he stipulated at the time of his sale, all while he was still by his master, but after the sale it is impossible to further stipulate. If the stipulation was while he was still by his master, a *goy*, he will be <u>like</u> a *Ger Toshav*, but not a total/real *Ger Toshav*, that behold, a real *Ger*

Toshav is only one who arouses himself and comes to 'l'heetgaire,' which is not so with this slave who was purchased from the *goy*, not from his own self did he come, and thus he is not a *Ger Toshav*. Rather since it is prohibited for a *Yisrael* to keep him in his home, one who has not accepted the Seven Laws, we can't entertain this unless he accepts upon himself that he will be **just <u>like</u>** a *Ger Toshav* in the manner of the laws.

Even so, he is <u>like</u> a *Ger Toshav* only that while he is in the house of a Jew, but if he is sold by the Jew to a new master, who is a *goy*, it is possible that he will return to the idolatry of his master. And if there is no proof of this matter, please consider Naaman, as it is said, 'May Hashem forgive your servant for this one thing, however; when my master comes to the temple of Rimmon to bow down there, he leans on my arm, so I must bow in the temple of Rimmon...' – the general rule is that a slave like this has not accepted upon himself commandments 'because they were commanded by God in the Torah and made known by Moshe Rabbeinu, that the *B'nai Noah* were commanded in them from before.[23] His entire acceptance is because his Israelite master forced it upon him, and behold, by him, these commandments are an aspect of servitude, and therefore he is only like a *Ger Toshav*, rather than a real *Ger Toshav*. And this is to say that it is written in *Hilchot Avadim* 'as he stands as a *goy*,' that this slave is only a '***goy who doesn't serve idols***' but he still has not left the status of *goy* completely.

Rather, it still remains necessary to clarify why it helps this condition, only in a slave that one purchases from a *goy*, and not a *goy* who sold himself? Surely, the first part of this *halacha* speaks about both of them! Therefore, Rabbeinu continues to explain that today we can only keep a slave that is **like a *Ger Toshav***, because such as this we cannot accept (*mekablin*) him, in fact to the contrary, behold we can force him into slavery. This matter is similar to what was ruled in *Hilchot Melachim* (10:3) with the youth who took a *mikvah* through *Bet din*: 'He is able to renege at the time of his maturity, and be ***Ger Toshav*** only.' But if he came to us in that we **should**

---

[23] *Hilchot Melachim* 8:11.

accept him and that he would then be *Ger Toshav*, whether as a son of free people or as a subordinate to Israel, **we can only accept one like this in a time of Yovel.**

It comes out that also while it is not a time of *Yovel*, there is a category similar to *Ger Toshav* – which is to say a slave that is <u>like</u> a *Ger Toshav*, with the addition of these two examples that were brought above, concerning the real *Ger Toshav* today.[24] However, in the case of this youth that took a *mikvah* through the guidance of the *Bet din,* which is similar in complete understanding to that of the slave, even if this youth was made into a real *Ger Toshav*, because the reason for their status is that they do not need us to accept them, that behold, their status is forced upon them. But it remains for us to clarify the first case that still hasn't been explained.

ב. *Ger Toshav* as a transitional stage to *Ger Tzedek*

We see proof from the language from Rabbeinu in *Hilchot Melachim* (10:3) where he speaks about *Ger Tzedek* – that

---

[24] *Hilchot Melachim* 9:1 & 10:3.

it speaks about what he was beforehand, *Ger Toshav*. In order to illuminate this complex matter, there is to look in *Hilchot Issurei Biah* (13:14) the place of commentaries of *Hilchot Geirus* in their categories:

> When a *Ger* or *Giuress* comes to convert – we check after them, lest they are coming for the sake of financial gain, or because they will merit a high-ranking position, or because of fear – have they come to enter into the Jewish Faith...and if we don't find any trespassing in them, we inform them of the weight of the yoke of Torah and the burden of doing it carried out by the simpletons/peoples of the world, as it is explained. If they accept it and do not turn away from it, and we see that they accepted it out of love – **accept them**.

Thus, are his words brought in the continuation of the *halachot*:[25]

> How do **we accept** *Gerei Tzedek*? When they come to convert we check after them and if we don't find any type of trespass, we say to them: 'What did you see that you

---

[25] ibid. 14:1.

came to convert? Don't you know that Israel today is very low and has pressured, swept up, pursued, and bothered situations coming on to them? [Should he say] I know and I am not worthy – accept him immediately.'

What is the meaning of the language 'we accept him immediately'? It is clear that it means we accept him to be stood up for conversion, and not that he was already made a *Ger*, that behold Rabbeinu continues:[26]

and we inform him of the fundamentals of Jewish Faith...and we inform him of the punishment of the commandments...if he returns and says I do not want to accept, he goes on his way, and if he does accept, we do not make him wait, rather we circumcise him immediately...and after that he enters the *mikvah*.'

Behold, we explain that before he enters into the Covenant, which is circumcision and *mikvah*, that with them, *Kedushat Yisrael* falls onto him - he is to stand with *Geirut Tzedek*. And in order to stand under *Geirus* – he needs to be accepted by *Bet din*. Should it not come to

___
[26] ibid. 2-4.

mind that *Bet din* will not accept someone who isn't careful with the rest of the commandments that were commanded to the *B'nai Noah*, that behold, if he wasn't careful in the commandments that he was obligated in from before, how will he fulfill many additional commandments?

This is why Rabbeinu wrote that *Bet din* 'checks after them' and if they 'see that he returned from Love' they 'accept him.' This means, if they see that they want to keep the commandments from Love, they are fit to stand for *Geirus*. It is clear that one who isn't careful in the Seven Laws – it is not possible to say upon him that he returned to Jewish Faith **from Love**! However, if it is clear that he was/is careful in the Seven Laws – and wants to add to them, we accept him as he stands.

And what happens if during his *Giur* he is cutoff in the middle of the process? And behold, the ruling is if he returned on it and didn't want to accept all of the commandments – 'he goes on his way.' Is it possible that he will leave it to go to idolatry? And what will his standing be if he doesn't convert fully?

It is hinted to us by Rabbeinu, in *Hilchot Melachim*, that every *Ger Tzedek* passes through the first category, *Ger Toshav*. Also, today we accept his standing as a complete

Geirus; we accept this like one who is accepted as a *Ger Toshav*. Rather, since today we don't accept one who wants to be *Ger Toshav* alone, therefore this *kabbalah* (acceptance) is limited to one who declares that he wants to be *Ger Tzedek* in the end. Therefore, we accept him, and his first category is *Ger Toshav*, and we move him along in order that he should be *Ger Tzedek*, but if for whatever reason he doesn't reach this, he will remain a *Ger Toshav*. But if he passes through the *Giur* and was already circumcised and has taken *mikvah*, and after that he wants to return from Hashem's ways **and to be a *Ger Toshav* alone as he was before**, ignore him.

ז. The Difference between *Chasid Umot HaOlam* and *Gerim Toshavim*

We see that one who comes to convert - we check after them if they came from Love, and this includes if he already keeps the Laws of Noah. This matter is explained in the words of Rabbeinu, even concerning one who comes to be *Ger Toshav* alone, thus are his words in *Issurei Biah* (14:7):

> Who is a *Ger Toshav*? This is a *goy* who accepts upon himself not to serve idols with the rest of the commandments commanded to the Sons of Noah, and was

not circumcised nor has taken a *mikvah*, **behold, this will cause him to be accepted, and he is a *Chasid* from the *Umot HaOlam.'***

It is explained that he has already accepted upon himself to keep the Seven Laws before *Bet din* has accepted him. However, basically, why do we need *Bet din* to accept him? Perhaps you can say, that we need a *Bet din* of three men, in front of which, he will accept the commandments, to keep the commandments as explained in *Hilchot Melachim* (8:10): 'And he needs to accept them before three men.' However, certainly *Bet din* can serve also for this function, but on this it is not possible to say **that they** are going to accept **him**. Rather that the explained matter is in the continuation of the *halacha* mentioned above:[27] 'And why do we call him '*Toshav?*' Because it is allowed for us to allow him to settle among us in the Land of Israel, just like we explained in *Hilchot Avodah Zara*. And we don't accept *Ger Toshav* except in a time of *Yovel Noheg*. But today, even if he accepted the entire Torah, except for one detail – we do not accept him.'

It comes out that we stand up an appropriate *Ger Toshav* as only one who requests permission to enter into the

---

[27] *Hilchot Issurei Biah* 14:7-8.

Land of Israel. One like this will mandate an acceptance of commandments before three, and even this needs *Bet din* to accept him. But most *goyim* don't have a specific desire to enter into the Land, and are not commanded to be *Gerim Toshavim*. However, they are commanded on Seven Laws of Noah, and if they accept them and do them because God commanded them in the Torah – behold, they are *Chasidei Umot HaOlam*.

Behold, Rabbeinu ruled in the complex matter of war in *Hilchot Melachim* (6:1): 'We don't make war with Men of the World until we call out to them in Peace...If they accept the Peace and accept the Seven Laws of Noah upon themselves – we don't kill even one soul of theirs.' Clearly, this does not mean that each one of them needs to accept before three men, therefore a matter like this needs an explicit explanation. The matter is explained in the continuation of his words in the complex matter of the covenant of Joshua with the Gibeonites. There, it is clear that only their messengers accepted by name, and even though this is so, it is considered as a *kabbalah* for all of them, and not only this, but it also allowed them to remain in the Land. It turns out that they stood as real *Gerim Toshavim*. Basically, how can we understand that this stood, after there wasn't a *kabbalah* before three men?

Rather it appears, just like as I explained above, that one who doesn't request to dwell in the Land of Israel doesn't need [*Bet din*] to be *Ger Toshav*; and all who accept upon themselves as the customs of the Nation to keep the Seven Laws, this is enough; and all those who fulfill them – behold they are *Chasidei Umot HaOlam*; and anything short of this is considered to be merely from their wise men; and these that don't fulfill them, they are judged by their peers that behold one of the Seven Laws is *dinim*. Even though the Gibeonites didn't request to remain in the Land, they were already there. All those who are already in the Land and keep the Seven Laws - they cannot be taken out, and behold their *din* is to be *Gerim Toshavim*, also without *kabbalah* before three men, and also without appearing before *Bet din*.

It is interesting that in *Hilchot Beit HaBechirah* (7:14) Rabbeinu rules that in Jerusalem '**we are not to place** in it *Ger Toshav*.' Why doesn't it just simply say 'don't place in it *Ger Toshav*?' However, this would contradict what it says in the tractate *Avodah Zara* (24b) that Aravnah the Jebusite – was a *Ger Toshav*, and behold, he was in Jerusalem. This *halacha* is based on what was commanded: 'He shall dwell with you in your midst; in a place that He will choose,'[28] and it is explained in *Sifri* 'to

---

[28]*Devarim* 23:17.

include *Ger Toshav,*' meaning that *Sifri* explains 'in one of your gates' – 'in your gates,' this is Jerusalem. This means that we are obligated to give *Ger Toshav* a place among us. After we accept them, this *kabbalah* obligates us to settle them in the Land. But this obligation is said of the rest of the Land, and not in Jerusalem, which is to say, as the Rambam stresses: 'we are not to give the *Ger Toshav* a place.' **We are not to give them** explicitly, but if he was already there, for example Aravnah the Jebusite, then certainly it is forbidden to remove him from there and we are to leave him there.

It should be mentioned regarding the *Yerushalmi Peah* (8:5):

> The Antebila Family was in Jerusalem and was related to Aravna the Jebusite. One time the sages ruled on them 600 *kikarei* of gold that was not to be taken out of Jerusalem, for they learned 'in your gates' – to include Jerusalem.

The *Pnei* Moshe explains: The sages learned two meanings of 'in your gates' that was written by the *Ger*: 'And you will be joyous by Hashem your God...and the Levite that is in your gate and the *Ger*,[29] and below it is written: 'and you

---

[29] *Devarim* 16:11.

will be joyous in your holiday...and the *Ger* and the orphan and the widow that is in your gate,[30] and to include Jerusalem that those who dwelled in its midst should not be taken out, and there you will give them a living...'

Behold, it speaks about later generations of families that would come out of Aravnah the Jebusite that still kept themselves <u>like</u> *Gerim Toshavim*, and since they were needy, the sages gave them plentiful support in order that they would be able to continue to dwell in the Holy City.

ה. The Obligation to Sustain *Gerim Toshavim*

Is there another aspect between the *Chasidei Umot HaOlam* and the *Ger Toshav* besides dwelling in the Land? In *Hilchot Avodah Zara* (10:2) Rabbeinu mentions in a passing manner: 'And *Ger Toshav* we are commanded to sustain them' – to give them free healthcare, and these matters are expanded in *Hilchot Melachim* (10:12): 'that we are accustomed with *Ger Toshav* with *Derech Eretz* and Kind Deeds like Israel...' and the source is what is written in *Vayikra* (25:35): 'And you will strengthen *Ger* and *Toshav* and he will he will live with you.'

---

[30] *Devarim* 16:14.

The Ramban already established this concept in his *Sefer HaMitzvot*[31] that Rabbeinu was to count this commandment like an additional commandment: 'to sustain *Ger Toshav*, that if he was drowning in a river or if heavy heap of ruins fell on top of him that it would take all of our strength to save him, and if he is sick we must involve ourselves with his medical recovery...even to the extent that if it is *pikuach nefesh* we must push off Shabbos.'

The Ramban suggests that perhaps Rabbeinu already included it within the commandment of *Tzedaka*.[32] How would this be, since it appears that according to the opinion of the Rambam, this obligation to sustain them falls only on one who is found among us, for example, one who has permission to dwell in the Land, or a youth who grew up in a Jewish household and was converted through *Bet din* and the like.; that behold, it should not rise in one's mind that Israel is obligated to seek out to each of the world's ends in order to sustain all of the *Chasidei Umot HaOlam* in each and every place?! However, certainly, if they were accepted, and permission was given to them to enter into the Land, just like we are commanded to give them a place to settle – then we are

---

[31] *Mitzvas Aseh* 16.

[32] *Aseh* 195.

obligated to sustain them, that behold, they are your brother, since they also fulfill the Seven Laws. From now on it appears that all who stand as *Ger Toshav*, and even today – you are 'commanded to sustain them.'

However, what is the *din* of those who keep the Seven Laws from the power of their own wisdom, and don't believe in the Creator of the World? The teaching of Rabbi Eliezer *Parasha Vav* explains: 'if they keep Seven Laws, and then they say...from their own intellect, this means that it was from their own intellect, or that they still believe in *shituf*...they only take their reward in this world.' Behold, this means that it reaches them in this world specifically – which is to say, we need to associate them with honor and moral support.

It is worthwhile to expound a little bit about these matters concerning the Seven Laws regarding 'from one's own intellect.' The Rambam explains in many places that there is for every man a natural sense of justice.

Thus, it says in *Moreh Nevuchim* 3:17:

> ...That the righteous is obligated, and it is necessary that God will be exalted. That is to say, that he is willing to obey all his good and honest deeds, even if they weren't commanded on them through the

medium of a prophet, and when he is punished over every evil deed that a man does, even if it is not forbidden to him through a prophet, for this is forbidden to him by his born nature; an implied prohibition of oppression and injustice.

And above ibid. 1:29:

Regarding the rebellion of the generation of the flood, it does not appear in the Torah that a prophetic messenger was sent unto them in that time, and nothing was forbidden unto them, and they were not threatened to be exterminated, it was said, about God that He was angry toward the people in His heart.

Also, the Generation of the Flood searched for meaning by themselves to avoid corruption. Seven Laws of Noah are the lower limit of natural morality that every man seeks out, because these prohibitions are placed into the hearts of the just, in order to feel them with one's intellect. However, there are many, many levels in the strength of Man's intellect. Also, the Nations of the World can possibly find the Higher Wisdom even without recognizing the Torah at all, since every man was created in the Image of

God and he is able to reach a high moral level. And thus, wrote the Rambam in the end of *Hilchot Shmittah* and *Yovel*:

> Each and every man from the population of the World that has a noble spirit in him, and understands from his own intellect how to separate and stand tall before Hashem, to minister to Him and to serve Him and to Know Hashem, going in a straight way just like God made him, and to remove from his neck the yoke of many calculations that sons of man request – behold, this will sanctify him as Holy of Holies, and Hashem will be his portion and his inheritance forever, and ever and ever.

It is basically clear that even one who is careful in the Seven Laws because of natural morality, and all the more so one who carries himself with a high level of morality and excellence until he goes in the just way, as God created him – certainly this is a great merit, such that he deserves to be saved on Shabbos. And because it is possible to consider that one who is sanctified as Holy of Holies, could it be forbidden to desecrate the Shabbos to sustain him?

The Rambam already wrote this in *Hilchot Shabbos* (2:3):

> ...The Laws of the Torah were not established in this world, except for the sake of mercy and kindness and peace in the world. And if the heretics will say that this is a desecration of the Shabbos and is forbidden - upon them it is written and says: 'And also I gave to them Statutes that were not Good and Laws that they could not live by.'[33]

However even those who serve idolatry, and those who are called by the language of the Rambam *'goyim,'* even upon them the Rambam ruled:[34] 'even *goyim*, God commanded to visit their sick, and to bury their dead with the dead of Israel, and to give livelihood to their poor – included with the poor of Israel, because of *Darkei Shalom*. Behold it is said, 'Her ways are comely ways and all of her paths are peaceful.'[35] And it does not need to be said that in a place one suspects his enemy and a hatred of Israel, the sages have already established:[36] *Nochrim* that are

---

[33] Ezekiel 20:25.

[34] *Hilchot Melachim* 10:12.

[35] *Mishlei* 3:17.

[36] *Hullin* 13:2.

outside the Land are not idolaters, rather, they handle the customs of their forefathers.' And since then, many of the peoples of the world have progressed a lot.

I. Conclusions based on the conclusions of the Rambam, and a brief discourse of the practical *halacha*:

1) All who fulfill the Seven Laws of Noah because God commanded them in Torah...Behold he is from the *Chasidei Umot HaOlam*. There is no need to check each and every one of them if in truth he accepted (*kabbalah*) upon himself the Seven Laws, rather since he belongs to the group, just like the Gibeonites, that their custom was to be obligated in the Seven Laws and to keep their *dinim* as fit – all of them have the *din* of *kosher B'nai Noah* from the *Chasidei Umot HaOlam*. And the Gaon Rabbi Moshe David Polsky in his *sefer Chemdas Yisrael b'kuntros Sheva Mitzvot*: 'One who governs himself from the day he is obligated in the commandments of *Ger Toshav*...Behold, he is categorically considered among *Gerim Toshavim*. Since he has not sinned – he does not need a new *kabbalah*.' And it is written further from HaRav Moshe Tzvi Chayot in his *Maamer Tiferet Yisrael 'Notzrim* that believe in Jewish Faith and in Torah from Heaven and the Reality of God and Reward in the World to

72

Come...without doubt their judgment by us is to be like *Ger Toshav*.' And it is written by GR'I Heinkin TZ'L: However also applicable to the nations of the world, if they call to Hashem God [of God's] it is written as a mention for the good. And it is already written that the *B'nai Noah* are not commanded against *shituf*, and simply the writings are as such, and only in a time when they settle in the Land of Israel must they separate completely from idolatry...and it is on us to seek out their peace. And it is beloved the Man who was created in God's image, and this is even of an idolater. And all the more so of the nations of the world of our times who don't serve idols. And all of the earlier generations, who uprooted idolatry from their hearts (and even those who bow to idols perhaps in our times by them it is a monument; this needs to be looked into). And it appears this is the reason that the law became easier and easier regarding the laws of *Nochrim* in the complex matter of renting houses and selling animals and benefitting from wine, etc. And even if there are idolaters among them, the vast majority of them in my opinion are categorically *Gerei Toshav*.

2) Those that keep the Seven Laws from the power of their own wisdom, they aren't believers that God

created the world, and upon them it is said, 'beloved is the man who was created in the divine image,' and we must develop a peaceful relationship with them, and at the very least we need to fulfill with them what the sages have said: 'that which is hateful to you, to another, do not do.'[37]

3) Even those who are idolaters, and those who are called *'goyim'* even on them the Rambam ruled:[38] 'Even *goyim*, the Sages commanded to visit their sick, bury their dead with the dead of Israel, and to provide livelihood for their poor alongside the poor of Israel, because of *Darkei Shalom*. Behold, it is said: 'Her ways are comely ways and all her pathways are of Peace.'[39] And it need not be said in a place that there is fear of an enemy or a hatred of Israel.

4) *Chasid Umot HaOlam* that accepts upon himself to keep the commandments before three, that they form a *Bet din*, and they accept him and they expand for him permission to enter the Land – behold, this is *Ger Toshav*.

---

[37] *Shabbos* 31a.

[38] *Hilchot Melachim* 10:12.

[39] *Mishlei* 3:17.

5) In general, we do not accept *Ger Toshav* accept in a time of *Yovel Noheg*. The reason is simple, because we are obligated to give them space to settle and all the while Israel isn't established on its own soil, each one in his inheritance, how do we give according to the obligation to settle others?

6) In what matters are we talking about when we say, 'that we don't accept *Ger Toshav* today'? With one whose needs that we have accepted, this is its meaning; one who still isn't established in the Land. But one who is already living in the Land, even in Jerusalem, if they only keep the Seven Laws - they have the *din* of *Ger Toshav*, and there are many like this. And look at what I've explained in the *SHU'T M'Lomdei Milchama* (43).

7) One who has already been accepted to stand with full *Geirus*, even outside the Land, but did not finish his *Geirus* – he remains *Ger Toshav* even today, that behold, we have obligated him since he was accepted to stand for *Geirus Tzedek*.

8) Thus, the *din* of the youth that received *Mikvah* for *Ger Tzedek* through *Bet din*, when he matures - he is able to choose to remain *Ger Toshav*, also today. Also, here the reason is because we have obligated him just like

we wanted to convert him through the guidance of the *Bet din.*

The 'Shahak affair' ... called a 'modern blood libel' by Rabbi Jakobovits in TRADITION's Summer 1966 issue ~ led to a responsum by Chief Rabbi Unterman of Israel stating that the Sabbath must be violated if necessary to save the lives of non-Jews as well as Jews. In this article, Rabbi Nachum Rabinovitch analyzes the basic legal concepts implicit in this responsum. Rabbi Rabinovitch's most recent contribution to these pages was his essay on '*Chametz* and *Matzah*' in our Spring 1966 issue.

Adaptation and Excerpts from

A Halakhic View of the Non-Jew

Rabbi Nachum Eliezer Rabinovitch

Purpose determines style. Thus, the manner of presentation and the organization of the arguments in a responsum are radically different from the approach used in a purely expository discussion. It is not only a matter of traditional practice, but often essential to the validity of the conclusions, that the style of a *Teshuvah* is usually what we might call inverted. One treats at length all the arguments that might be advanced against the conclusion to be established; the most far-fetched negative argument is eliminated first, and one proceeds until all are rejected. The intended decision then remains as the only possibility, and the arguments for it are often dismissed in just a few words.

The purpose of a responsum is not primarily to explain why the law holds in a particular case. It is, rather, to prove that no matter how we look at a particular issue, the decision could not be otherwise. Thus, one accepts for the sake of argument hypotheses, which are not really justified, in order to show that even if they were, the validity of the decision would be not affected. Naturally, when it comes to explaining the real motivations for the decision, the responsum may be downright misleading because the positive reasons for the law may not be adequately stressed.

By way of illustration, we might refer to the infamous Shahak affair, which has been in the news in recent months. Figuring prominently in the discussion evoked by this modern libel is a responsum by the Ashkenazi Chief Rabbi I. J. Unterman, which has been widely quoted and just as widely misconstrued. In view of the prevalent ignorance of Jewish Law, with respect to this sensitive area, it might be advisable to present an outline of the main halakhic issues involved. To sum up the Biblical attitude to man, the *Mishnah* quotes R. Akiva: 'Beloved is man for he was created in the image of God. Out of special love it was made known to him that he was created in the Divine image.' Rabbi Akiva goes on to describe the uniqueness of Israel in choosing to acknowledge its Father in Heaven, thereby meriting the status of 'children of the Lord your God,'[40] and qualifying for the precious gift of Torah.

Rashi comments: 'Beloved is man . . . therefore it is his duty to do his Maker's will.' For Israel, 'our Maker's will' is expressed in the 613 commandments. What about the rest of mankind? Basing itself on Biblical references and historical tradition, the Talmud lists 'Seven Commandments of the sons of Noah.' These apply equally to all mankind, since Noah was the progenitor of all. Of these, six are prohibitions and one is mandatory. The one positive commandment is to set up an administration of justice to enforce the other six commandments as well as such other just and equitable laws as may be enacted by suitable authority.

Forbidden are: 1) murder, 2) incest, 3) robbery, 4) eating the flesh of animals which are still alive, 5) idolatry and 6) blasphemy.

Jews are subject to many more commandments, including those which set forth their obligations to their fellow-men, in general, and fellow Jews, in particular. Clearly, every human being is equally stamped with the image of God. Nonetheless, it is clear that my obligations to a man living half-way across the world, whom I will never see, ought not to be the same as those to my immediate neighbor. If they are set forth as the same, then they

---

[40] *Devarim* 14: 1.

certainly cannot amount to very much! Clearly, too, my responsibilities to my fellow man ought to vary according to his circumstances as well as mine. One who is undernourished because he is rich and stingy cannot claim the same assistance as one who is starving because of poverty. If I happen to be a doctor, it is my obligation to care for the sick; but if know nothing about medicine, treating certain diseases is not only not my duty, it is in fact forbidden, since in my ignorance, I am likely to do more harm than good.

Furthermore, a community, like an individual, undertakes certain special obligations to one who is invited as a guest. Yet not everybody can lay claim to the right to be invited lest the multitude of guests eat their host out of home and hearth. Recognizing these distinctions, the *Halacha* divides mankind into three broad categories according to the commandments they are subject to and the obligations Jews have towards them.

1. Son of Noah, subject to the Seven Commandments.
2. *Ger Toshav* (resident alien) - a Son of Noah who has been granted residence rights in the Jewish State. While any fugitive slave who accepts the Seven Commandments must be admitted to residence in the Holy Land,[41] others are admitted only on condition that they are accepted by a tribunal of three, before whom

---

[41] *Devarim* 23: 16, 17.

they declare their willingness to abide by the Seven Commandments.

'Why is he called *Toshav* (resident)? Because it is permitted for us to settle him among us in the Land of Israel.' The *Ger Toshav*, like the fugitive slave, is entitled to more than just admission to the country. To both applies the mandate of the Torah: 'He shall dwell with you, in the midst of you, in the place which he shall choose within one of your gates, as it pleases him; you shall not vex him.'[42] This commandment is especially relevant.

The Rabbis explain 'in the place which he shall choose' – where his livelihood is to be found; 'in one of your gates'– he is not to be set wandering from place to place.' The residents of the town may not complain that he is competing with them in order to force him to move on. On the contrary, they are obligated to sustain him. Thus, the immigrant is entitled to the assistance of the Jewish community to establish himself and his family.

This law applies only under the ideal conditions of Jewish independent statehood. 'A *Ger Toshav* is

---

[42] *Devarim* loco cit.

accepted only when the Jubilee is in operation.' However, at any time 'anyone who keeps the Seven Commandments may not be excluded from dwelling in the land, although the court does not have jurisdiction to accept him.'

3. The third category consists of Jews, who are completely responsible for one another.

Except for granting of immigrants' privileges, our obligations to a Son of Noah in our midst are the same as those to a *Ger Toshav* and are applicable to the Diaspora. Especially important is the Biblical injunction:[43] 'If your brother falls low and cannot maintain himself with you, you shall uphold him; though be he a stranger (*Ger*) or a resident (*Toshav*) he shall live with you.' The *Sifra* understands *Ger* as a proselyte or complete convert to Judaism and *Toshav* as a resident alien.

What is implied in 'He shall live with you?'

Nachmanides in his Bible commentary explains:

It is a mandatory commandment to sustain him. This is the source of the positive commandment to save a life. Based on this the Rabbis said: 'Your brother shall live with you.'[44] Ben Petura

---

[43] *Vayikra* 25:35.
[44] ibid. 36.

explained this verse: If two are travelling in the desert and (only one of them has a jug of water so that if he drinks he will be able to reach an inhabited place, but if both drink, both will die (since the water supply is inadequate), said Ben Petua, 'Better that they both drink and die and let neither one see the other die.' Rabbi Akiva, however, taught: 'Your brother shall live with you – your life takes precedence over your fellow's life.' The repetition of 'your brother shall live with you'[45] emphasizes the command.

Although Maimonides does not consider this verse[46] as the source of the commandment to save a life, he does not disagree with the interpretation of the intent of this passage, for he rules that 'since we are commanded to sustain a *Ger Toshav*, he must be given medical treatment without charge.'

Is there any difference between our obligation to save the life of a Jew and a *Ger Toshav*? The *Sifra*, to which Nachmanides refers, is explicit. There are two passages enjoining us to sustain life: one refers to a *Ger Toshav*, the other, to 'your brother,' namely, a Jew. The interpretation that the word 'with' (in 'he shall live with you' and 'your brother shall live with you') implies that in extremity

---

[45] Verse 36.

[46] Verse 35 alone nor both 35 and 36.

your life takes precedence over his, is expressly stated in *Sifra* in both instances. Thus, were it not for the limitation inherent in the word 'with,' one would suppose that you must be ready to give your life for a *Ger Toshav* no less than for a full Jew. Now that the Torah gives your life precedence, it precedes the life of your *Toshav*. In other words, our obligation to save a life is exactly the same for a *Ger Toshav* as for a Jew and requires that we do everything short of sacrificing our own to save him.

What if there is a conflict of duties? If saving a life involves a major transgression does duty takes precedence in such a case?

For a son of Noah, the question is irrelevant. With the exception of murder, 'A son of Noah who is compelled to transgress one of his commandments is permitted to do so; even if he is compelled to worship idols, he may do so, because he is not commanded to sanctify God's name,' nor even to worship Him.

A Jew, however, is subject to the command, 'You shall not profane my holy Name, but I will be sanctified among the people of Israel.'[47] The Talmud establishes that idolatry, incest, and murder may not be committed, even to save one's life. A Jew Is required to sanctify the name of God by martyrdom rather than transgress these commandments. Even with respect to other

---

[47] *Vayikra* 22:32.

commandments, martyrdom is required under certain circumstances.

Generally, however, a commandment may be transgressed in order to save human life. What is the source of this rule? In *Yoma* 85a we read of a discussion on this point between Rabbi Ishmael, Rabbi Akiva, Rabbi Elazar ben Azariah, and others. Their primary concern was with the Sabbath, since the Sabbath is a keystone of Torah, included in the Tablets of the Covenant, and, in some respects, desecrating the Sabbath is equivalent to idolatry.

The scriptural source of this law is the verse:[48] 'You shall therefore keep my statutes and my ordinances, which if a man do, he shall live by them and not die by them.' Now, who is the subject of this clause, 'which if a man does he shall live'? Does 'man' refer to a Jew or to any man? The Talmud several times quotes Rabbi Meir: 'How do we know that even a non-Jew who occupies himself with the Torah is like the High Priest? For it is written 'which if a man does he shall live' – not Priests, Levites, or Israelites, but MAN. Thus, you learn that even a non-Jew who engages in the Torah is like a High Priest.'

The Talmud concludes that this refers to the Seven Commandments, since a non-Jew is not obligated for the rest. Thus, it is clear that the verse which authorizes desecrating the

---

[48] *Vayikra* 18:5.

Sabbath in order that a man may live refers to any son of Noah, not just to Jews. Nachmanides formulates the laws in the following manner: We are commanded to sustain a *Ger Toshav*, to save him from harm, e.g., if he be drowning in a river or if a ruin fell on him, we must try with all our power to save him. If he be sick, we must treat him. For one of our brothers, an Israelite, or a proselyte (*Ger Tzedek*), we are certainly obligated to him in all these things. This is for them 'saving a life which suspends the Sabbath.' This is what the Almighty says: 'If your brother falls low and cannot maintain himself with you, you shall uphold him; though he be a stranger or a resident he shall live with you,' and in the Talmud they said: 'You are commanded to sustain a *Ger*' . . . and this commandment was counted by the author of *Halachot* as 'Sustain thy brother,' but the master (Maimonides) includes it with charity, commandment number 195 . . . but in fact they are two separate commandments.

Considerable literature deals with the conditions under which medical treatment is permissible on the Sabbath. Before proceeding to discuss particulars, Maimonides states the general rule.

> As regards a dangerously ill person, the Sabbath is like a weekday for all things that he requires. It is forbidden to delay breaking the Sabbath for one dangerously ill, as it is written 'which if a man do,

he shall live and not die.' Thus, you learn that the laws of the Torah are not for vengeance against the world, but for compassion, loving kindness and peace in the world. As for those heretics (the Karaites) who say it is a desecration of the Sabbath and forbidden ~ about them scripture says: 'Moreover I gave them statutes that were not good and ordinances by which they could not have life.'[49]

What about childbirth? On the one hand, delivering a baby involves no Biblically prohibited form of work. On the other hand, childbirth is a natural function of a healthy mother. There is nothing pathological or dangerous in ordinary cases.

But for the mother's peace of mind and comfort it may be necessary to perform activities that entail a violation of the Sabbath. They, too, are permitted, but with the proviso that, if at all possible, they be done differently from the usual method so that technically they will no longer be in the category of Biblically prohibited forms of work. Thus, even for a blind woman, it is permitted to kindle a light, so that she will feel reassured that those attending her can see clearly and look after her needs.

---

[49] Ezekiel 20:25.

Accordingly, Maimonides maintains that for a woman in childbirth 'whatever is possible to do differently must be done so. 'But in the case of a dangerously sick person he writes 'the Sabbath is like a weekday for all things that he requires,' and one need not modify the normal manner of performing the activity. Although the obligation to treat a *Ger Toshav* is expressly stated, when Maimonides speaks of suspending the Sabbath to save a life, neither Jew nor *Toshav* are mentioned. In his discussion of childbirth, a distinction is made between a Jew and a *Toshav*.

'We deliver a woman *Ger Toshav*, since we are commanded 'to sustain him,' but one must not violate the Sabbath for her.' Obviously, since for a woman in childbirth, a change from the usual procedure is required, for a non-Jew the indicated change is to have a non-Jew assist if necessary, and he will be able to do his work in the normal manner. However, there is no question that insofar as the actual delivery is concerned, this duty is implicit in the commandment 'to sustain him,' and a Jew should not relinquish the opportunity to perform this *Mitzvah*. In fact, if no non-Jew is available, even the other services may be done by a Jew with a suitable change of procedure, since technically there will then be no Biblically prohibited Sabbath work.

The Jew accepts gratefully the responsibilities imposed upon him to respect the Divine image in man and make every sacrifice, barring only life itself, to save the life of another. However, does this obligation extend to criminals who rebelliously cast off the

Divine image? Although we are not ordinarily permitted to take the law into our own hands to attack wrongdoers (except to save a victim or other special cases) 'if harm comes to habitual criminals of itself, we are not commanded to save them.'

In the long and troubled history of the Jewish People, it has been our lot at different times to be exposed to savage and wicked peoples whose religion was violence and whose law was murder, rape, and plunder. In speaking of some of the Roman occupation officials, the *Mishnah* warns against seeing one of them unescorted, and certainly putting oneself in their hands for medical treatment, because one would never come out of the encounter alive. And in our own twentieth century, brutes like Mengele and his battalions of German doctors devised fiendish ways of utilizing modern medical techniques to sterilize, maim, and slaughter helpless Jews.

Yet even in dealing with such abominable creatures, the Rabbis felt that to refrain from helping them in their time of need could not be justified. They were concerned about the danger of fanning the flames of hatred to an even higher pitch and, more importantly, their innate optimism about man's better-self led them to hope that by our pursuit of 'the ways of peace,' even wild beasts might be tamed. To this end, even desecration of the Sabbath was permitted when necessary. This is to be done with the awareness that the name of God will be glorified in this function and in the hope that in the hearts of all his creatures there will be awakened the desire to serve Him.

Yet, such is the ethical sensitivity of the *Halacha*, that even in the presence of the danger which might ensue from aggravated hatred, the Talmud is concerned about the rightness of helping bring into the world an innocent baby when it is known that he will be raised as a brute and will be brought up to disregard the most elementary attributes of humanity. Today, we are concerned about the moral rectitude of opposing birth control when children are born fated to starve. Is there not at least an equal basis for anxiety when children are brought into the world to serve as cannon fodder or as the spiritually blind shock troops of a mad emperor?

If proof were needed that the vast majority of non-Jews should be accorded the treatment of a *Ger Toshav*, it might be appropriate to cite the views of some of the classical and modern *halakhic* authorities.

In his Talmud commentary, Meiri writes:

> All who hold to the Seven Commandments are treated equally in the law with us and there is no favoritism for us. It goes without saying that this is so for the nations who are disciplined in the ways of religions and civilization.

Why does it go without saying? Simply because the great religions demand even more than just the Seven Commandments. Meiri continues:

> The Almighty will not deprive anyone of reward who engages in Torah for its own sake. It has been expressly said: 'Even a non-Jew who engages in Torah, even only in his Seven Commandments, and even if his nation, as a whole, transgresses them, since, however, he fulfills them as the Creator's command, he is like the High Priest.' Moreover, with regard to other commandments, the Almighty will not deprive of reward those who fulfill them – even for a becoming expression, even for hurrying to perform a *Mitzvah* though it be not such as needs to be done immediately. It is a great principle for all His commandments: According to a man's works, so shall he be rewarded.

In a monograph, which appeared in 1840, Rabbi Zvi Chayes discusses at length Jewish-Gentile relations. We quote here only one paragraph:

> The Seven Commandments are the natural laws which both Christians and Mohammedans apply in their courts, and both see that they are fulfilled . . . and everyone who keeps the Seven

Commandments, because they were given in God's Torah by the hand of Moses, is a *Ger Toshav*. Also, Maimonides (Laws of Kings 12) and the *Kuzari* (4: 34) write that these religions are a prelude and a preparation for the hoped-for Messiah, who is the principal fruit. Then they will all become his fruit when they acknowledge Him and the tree will become whole and they will hold dear the root which they despised at first.

A leading *Posek* (*halachic* authority) of our day, Rabbi Joseph Eliyahu Henkin writes: 'Beloved is man for he was created in the image of God.' This applies even to idolaters.[50] Certainly, the people of the world in our time are not idol worshippers.

And with the passage of the generations, idolatry has been progressively uprooted from their hearts . . . and even if there are some who worship idols, in my opinion, the overwhelming majority are in this category. As for the rule in the Talmud[51] that a *Ger Toshav* must accept the Seven Commandments before a tribunal of three, as a decree from God through Moses, this is only with respect to our obligation to provide him with a livelihood and the privilege to reside in the Land of Israel. But, insofar as being removed from the class of idolaters is concerned, anyone

---

[50] See *Tiferet Israel* on *Avot*.

[51] *Yevamot* 46, *Avodah Zarah* 64.

who denies idolatry and acknowledges that the Seven Commandments are obligatory, is a *Ger Toshav*.

When a Rabbi in Israel writes a responsum to a question dealing with our responsibilities to a non-Jew, all of the background material we have discussed is taken for granted. Without it, one cannot begin to understand what the responsum is all about.

For centuries, we were besieged and beleaguered, hounded and persecuted. Every diabolical stratagem was applied to destroy the spirit and the body of those who remained loyal. And yet we survived – not, as might be expected, embittered and hardened beyond the capacity for humane feeling and compassion. Not so! Our fathers, who suffered in the ghettos of the middle ages and the pale of Russia, and our brothers, who in our own day felt the satanic fury of accursed Nazidom, were not brutalized by the enormity of their suffering.

The more they suffered, the deeper did Jews penetrate to the meaning of the *Halacha* about man and the more truly did their day-to-day practice reflect the highest response to God's imperative. Compassion and mercy for all men are the mark of the Jew, just as they are of God. As Rabbi Akiva said, 'Beloved is man for he was created in the image of God. . . . Beloved is Israel for they are called 'children of God,' '

Conclusion
One [Potential] Noahide; Two [Actual] Paths

~~

By Rabbi David Katz

Based on the *Psak* of the Lubavitcher Rebbe on Rambam's *Ger Toshav*[52] (*Ger Chasid*)

Today's righteous Gentile walks along a spiritual path much the same as any other true believer of any other faith. 'The Path' is cliché, but since the Torah is the *kosher* path, according to its own true believers, the *kosher* path [not surprisingly] has found its 'fork in the road.' The Noahide plight would go something like this:

The Road Not Taken

by Robert Frost

Two roads diverged in a yellow wood,
And sorry I could not travel both
And be one traveler, long I stood
And looked down one as far as I could
To where it bent in the undergrowth;

Then took the other, as just as fair,
And having perhaps the better claim,
Because it was grassy and wanted wear;
Though as for that the passing there
Had worn them really about the same,

---

[52] Rambam *Hilchot Melachim* 8:10-11.

And both that morning equally lay
In leaves no step had trodden black.
Oh, I kept the first for another day!
Yet knowing how way leads on to way,
I doubted if I should ever come back.

I shall be telling this with a sigh
Somewhere ages and ages hence:
Two roads diverged in a wood, and I—
I took the one less traveled by,
And that has made all the difference.

If you ask a Noahide what a Noahide is and where it comes from [by today's standards], he would most certainly answer you: 'a Noahide keeps the Seven Laws of Noah, and it comes from the Torah.' If you ask an educated and invested Orthodox Jew, you will get roughly the same answer, the only significant difference being that a Rabbi may quote to you the Rambam as the source of Noahism in practice, citing the exact source, if you are lucky.

The Rambam sources the main ingredients of the path of the righteous gentile as follows:

Hilchot Melachim: 8:10-11

10 Moses only gave the Torah and *mitzvot* as an inheritance to Israel, as *Devarim* 33:4 states: 'The Torah... is the inheritance of the congregation of Jacob,' and to all those who desire to become *Ger* from among the other nations, as *Bamidbar* 15:15 states ' the *Ger* shall be the same as you.' However, someone who does not desire to accept Torah and *mitzvot*, should not be forced to.

By the same regard, Moses was commanded by the Almighty to compel [L'Chof] all the inhabitants of the world to accept the commandments given to Noah's descendants.

If one does not accept these commands, he should be executed. A person who formally accepts these commands is called Ger Toshav in every place. This acceptance [Kabbalah] must be made in the presence of three Haverim.

Anyone who agrees to circumcise himself and allows twelve months to pass without circumcising himself is considered as one of the nations.

11   Anyone who accepts [*Kabbalah*] upon himself the fulfillment of these seven *mitzvot* and is precise in their observance is considered one of 'From the *Chasidei Umot HaOlam*' and will merit a share in the world to come.

This applies only when he **accepts them and <u>fulfills</u>** them because the Holy One, blessed be He, commanded them in the Torah and informed us through Moses, our teacher, that Noah's descendants had been commanded to fulfill them previously.

However, if he fulfills them out of intellectual conviction, he is not a *Ger Toshav*, nor of 'From the *Chasidei Umot HaOlam*,' nor of their wise men.

In this Rambam we find four essential components that will mold the path of the righteous gentile:

1. The Noahide requirements
2. *Chasid* requirements
3. *Ger Toshav* requirements
4. *Bet din* requirements

Although these two *halachot* in this Rambam source offer an immense amount of information concerning Gentiles and their path to righteousness, we will focus on these *four fundamentals* with their source and context in the Oral Torah tradition.

The Noahide

If you are involved with Noahides today, then it would be safe to assume that you are familiar with the Lubavitcher Rebbe, and his association with Noahism. For all intents and purposes, he invented the contemporary version of it, at least as far as Orthodox involvement goes. There is a clear and well-established bond between 'Noahide' and 'The Rebbe.' The Rebbe wrote and spoke about Noahide and its obvious Messianic relevance, and he established the proper *halachot* to follow, by adhering to our aforementioned Rambam. In short,

The Rebbe laid out the: who, what, when, where, how, and why of Noahide, according to Torah, and we undoubtedly follow in the footsteps of The Rebbe when it comes to understanding Noahide Torah.

The Rebbe's Noahide slightly changed in shape and form over the decades, ultimately becoming something even more dynamic than the archetype Noahide that The Rebbe knew in the legend that was Dr. Vendyl Jones. By the time of the Rebbe's passing in 1994, the Noahide path was grafted back into civilization and into the consciousness of anyone who would come to look into what it means to be a 'Light to Nations.' The internet set this new movement into motion, and soon the cyber truth-seeker would easily be able to find numerous websites and online organizations who were setup to help Noahides on their path, continuing the work of The Rebbe. The most notable in specific is AskNoah.org, an online organization, who after compiling 'The Divine Code: a *Shulchan Aruch* for Noahides,' partnered up with '*Pirchei Shoshanim*,' another online organization that specializes in teaching *Shulchan Aruch* studies. The rally cry for this team is to put all Noahides and Jews in teaching positions on the same page, teach uniformity in the Noahide Laws, and pave the path going forward. If the Rebbe was the father of the Noahide Movement, this team thought to become its official institution.

The Divine Code theology works off the following principles:

(which in theory would work, and provide a safe and *kosher* path for all to walk on, however the problem with this ideology, is that to achieve its success, those who created this path [*shita*] deliberately changed the established *halacha* [of the Rambam, and therefore the Rebbe].)

- A Noahide is an *acum* [idolater]
- A Noahide is a *Shabbos Goy*
- There is not a possibility of any type of *Ger* or *Ger Toshav*; only a full convert – *Ger Tzedek*
- Divine Code is the established *halacha* for Noahides, undisputed, and follows the *halacha* as it exists historically
- The Rambam is the *halacha*, and the Word of God
- *The Divine Code* is a translation of its original work, *Sheva Mitzvot Hashem*, authored by Rabbi Moshe Weiner
- *Ger* means convert; *Ger Toshav* means resident alien
- The Rambam, who mentions *Ger Toshav*, is referring to a *Ger Toshav* in the Land at a time of Jubilee
- *Ger Toshav* today would be a type of partial conversion
- *Ger Toshav* is considered making a new religion
- *Ger Toshav* requires a *Bet din*
- A Noahide cannot reject *shituf* [with *kabbalah*]

- All contemporary sources and understandings of *Chazal* follow this reasoning and understanding
- *The Divine Code* is the only *Shita*
- The Rebbe never mentioned *Ger*
- All sources are contrived to follow a consistent view, predicated on 'no *Ger Toshav* until Jubilee'
- *Gemara Arachin* 29a speaks about all *Ger Toshav*
- There is only one kind of gentile; a Noahide gentile keeps the Seven Laws
- A Noahide who wants more than Seven Laws is encouraged to convert to Judaism
- The other *shita* implies that a *Ger Toshav* status is mandatory, thus problematic (the conclusion of *V'Shav HaKohen*)

Granted the neo-Noahide [post-Rebbe] Path is a safe, non-threatening [theoretical] option, but it cannot be taken seriously, nor trusted. It is outside of the tradition and it only came into existence through forgery, an exploitation of the most crucial aspects of the *halacha* [of the Rambam].

The Rebbe and The Rambam

The Rebbe explains the Rambam with refreshing clarity, and by the end of the Rebbe's *psak*, two clear paths emerge. One is Noahide, and the other is *Ger* [*Toshav*]. One does not negate the other; both are valid options, when in context, and neither come through a compromise of the Rambam's *halacha*. In fact, the Rebbe elucidates the Rambam in accordance with all Rabbis, who either wrote on the subject or have come to explain the Rambam. The Rebbe gives us the *halacha* in harmony.

The following are fundamental points from the Rambam's *halacha,* in light of the Rebbe [the *psak* of the Rebbe]:

- *Ger Toshav* does NOT imply Jubilee
- A *Bet din* of three men is NOT mandatory
- We should strive to make Noahides
- When the opportunity arises to make a *Ger Chasid* it is an extremely important *mitzvah* to do so
- A Noahide is characterized by one who fulfills the Seven Laws with proper intentions.
- A *Ger Chasid* is characterized, not only through fulfilling the Seven Laws, but by properly accepting them as well [with proper intent]. This acceptance is the acceptance of the yoke of heaven, which is not incumbent on the Noahide. A Noahide is commanded to not serve other gods, while the *Ger* proactively accepts belief in God.
- A *Ger Toshav* [here] is one who has taken *kabbalah*, and is then referred to as a *Chasid*...for he is careful with the Seven Laws. The *kabbalah* is called *Ger Toshav,* and the aftermath is *Chasid*...[hence *Ger Chasid*]

- The Rebbe clearly states this *Ger Toshav* is not a type of conversion, and it is a very limited use of the term, applicable only to the nature of the *kabbalah*.
- There is no fear of making a new religion.
- This is consistent with the Rebbe's views of *Ger Toshav* [see *Likutei Sichot* vol. 31 *Mishpatim*]
- The Rebbe shows how, not only the Rambam held this way, but that this is the accepted *shita* of a known '*Ger Toshav sugia.*' There are no other views on how this *sugia* works or on how it is implemented.
- The Rebbe acknowledges that there are two paths: Noahide – where the *Ger* path is inapplicable for any reason, and the *Ger Chasid* path – which the Rebbe encouraged, calling it a tremendous *mitzvah*, one applicable for all of time [based on opportunity].
- The Rebbe states we don't follow the conclusions of *V'Shav HaKohen*, according to *halacha*.

Key Components to Rambam.

1) Noahide = One who fulfills Seven Laws of Noah with proper intention.
2) *Chasid* = One who not only fulfills the Seven Laws, but does so after taking a proper *kabbalah*.

3) *Ger Toshav* = One who accepts properly [*kabbalah*] the yoke of heaven as a prerequisite of becoming a *Chasid*; not to be confused with the *halachic* [Jubilee] *Ger Toshav*.

4) *Bet din* = One should stand before three Jewish scholars; in this case it is not imperative, but if performed it will grant one the honorary title of *Ger* [*Toshav*] along with *Chasid* [*Ger Chasid*].

Standing Before Three Scholars [*Talmud Bavli, Yerushalmi Talmud*]

The mandate to come before three scholars [a lesser, more common *Bet din*] is sourced in the *Yerushalmi Talmud*, in conjunction to protecting the sanctity of The Land of Israel in a time of the Temple. In Temple times [after the return from Bavel] the Jewish People needed a secure system to ensure *kashrut* over all Torah living, especially concerning produce and its relevant laws. The system called for the lesser educated to come before a tribunal of three scholars, upon which they would show scholarship and be deemed reliable/trustworthy. The term for this *kashrut* is '*mekablin*' which roughly implies 'on the same page [with the scholars].'

A *Ger Toshav* at the time of the Temple must keep the Seven Laws of Noah, go before the tribunal, and come out '*mekablin.*' This would ensure that the *Ger Toshav* [non-Jew] could be trusted in holy matters that are vital for Jewish survival [when interacting with non-Jews]. This is called *'Yovel Noheg'* – a standard level of observance that one would be knowledgeable to operate even in a time of Jubilee [which to function on a Jubilee level, a certain degree of knowledge is mandatory]. Thus, the terms *'Ger Toshav'* – *'Yovel'* – *'Bet din,'* etc. refer to this type of *Ger Toshav.*[53] It is a *Yerushalmi* concept, and it is mentioned in the *Bavli* in select discussions. There are many other instances when the *Bavli* speaks in *Yerushalmi* terms.

Avodah Zara 64b asks: 'who is a *Ger Toshav*' and the *halacha* is expressed as expected: Seven Laws, stand before three scholars, etc. This is the *Bavli* speaking in *Yerushalmi* terms; the concepts are borrowed. The reason for the borrowing is because the *Ger Toshav* concept works in *Bavli* matters. For example, how do I know if a non-Jew can touch Jewish wine? The *halacha* is that they can if they are *Ger Toshav*, and the standard is laid out in the *Bavli* through borrowing from the *Yerushalmi*. The outcome is the same: a non-Jew who can be relied upon/trusted. People who are quick to point out that we are not in a time of Jubilee, are making a mistake through unawareness of the *Ger Toshav sugia*. The Rambam[54] quotes from *Arachin* [about *Ger Toshav* only in a time of Jubilee], but only says we are not *mekablin* [them]. This means that the *Yerushalmi* level of *Ger Toshav* is not applicable until a time of Jubilee, but a lesser *Bavli* version

---

[53] *Arachin* 29a, *Bechorot* 30

[54] *Issurei Biah* 14:8.

of *Ger Toshav* isn't only applicable[55] today, it is a major aspect of *halacha* and the basis of all Jewish interactions with our non-Jewish neighbors.

The Rebbe's *Shita*

The Rebbe makes clear, not only the path of the Noahide and how to make Noahides, but also the path of the *Ger [Toshav]* and the *mitzvah* of making *Gerim*. The Rebbe points out that a *Ger Toshav* [singular] in the Rambam is different than taking oath to be *Gerim Toshavim* [plural]. The difference is that the former implies the borrowed language/concepts for the sake of the oath, and the latter would imply becoming actual *Gerim Toshavim,* as spoken of in the *Yerushalmi* which can't take place unless it is a time of Jubilee. In short, the Rambam's usage/context/meaning [copy and paste from *Chazal*] is uniquely and distinctly different from the *Yerushalmi Ger Toshav* in every way. There are simply two types of *Ger Toshav* at play here, and with deep focus on *Ger Toshav*, one will actually find not only many types of *Ger Toshav*, but many types of *'Ger[im]'* as well.

The Rebbe taught the Noahide world how to cultivate Noahides, and he also revealed the nuances of *Ger Toshav*; he advocated and encouraged both. Through the Rebbe we see one cannot

---

[55] Rambam *Issurei Biah* 14:7.

exist without the other; both are necessary, and each is a unique aspect of Oral Torah. It should be noted, that the Rebbe's Noahide [*shita*] does not contradict the *Ger Toshav*, for *Ger Toshav* in the Rambam is not of *Yovel*, and this does not contradict or complicate the Noahide path. The Noahide and the *Ger Toshav* are two completely separate entities within the Rambam. The Rambam carries many *shitot* within this *halacha*,[56] and this is not unique in the Rambam, rather, this is the style of the Rambam.

Today's Noahide *shita* stands categorically against the Rebbe's *shita* of Noahide, and even worse, it denies *Ger Toshav* through misrepresenting the Rambam [as speaking of Jubilee]. This produces two *shitot* in the Noahide world today: one that stands with the Rebbe [vis a vis the Rambam] which is to say that Noahides can exist, or choose to progress into a *Ger Chasid*, and one that represents a false Noahide, albeit well-intentioned. The major practical difference between the two *shitot* is a Noahide only rejects idolatry but may still engage in *shituf*. In fact, without being *Ger Toshav*, they are *halachically acum*, are in the category of *Shabbos Goy*, and are still considered as worshipping *b'shituf*. The proponents of this *shita* are open about this *halachic* standing when questioned, however they conceal it from its adherents. The *Ger Toshav shita* stands in direct opposition on these points, and most crucial of all, takes a

---

[56] *Hilchot Melachim* 8:10-11.

proactive belief in God, shedding the *shituf* label for those who stand attached to Israel. The *Ger Toshav shita* understands that the Noahide path must exist, even if it is only a step on the path. However, the neo-Noahides reject the *Ger Toshav shita*.

It should be noted, that the fear of the neo-Noahide *shita* is 'lest the *Ger Toshav* be guilty of making a new religion.' The prohibition of making a new religion is a preventative measure to ensure that a non-Jew should not establish a new *mitzvah* with intention of performing it as a Jew. This would be akin to making an eighth Noahide Law, and the penalty of doing so is severe. The Torah example of such behavior is a non-Jew keeping Shabbos like a Jew, i.e. thirty-nine *Melachot*. The *Ger Toshav* do, however, keep a lesser Shabbos that sees them perform *melacha* per force; their goal is to believe in Hashem and not do *melacha* for a Jew, to which would be akin to returning to the idolatry that they have already rejected.[57]

What is a *Ger*?

In today's world, a *Ger* is a convert. In *Chazal*'s world, a *Ger* carried several meanings: alien, stranger, convert, sojourner, dweller, slave, worker, *baal teshuva*, Noahide, resident alien, etc. Our *Poskim* called Noahides '*Gerim*,' but due to pains of exiles, their number were considerably small compared to the

---

[57] *Rashi Yevamot* 48b.

number of full-fledged converts over the last thousand years. But we were promised that in the End of Days there would be *Gerim Grurim*, non-Jews who would return to the Torah, even in a time when the Jews are ill-equipped to accept these *Gerim*. One cannot deny that these times are upon us, and the obvious problems that have risen out of this are: 'confusion over who or what is a *Ger*' and 'are we capable of taking Noahide to the next level.' The truth of the matter is: a convert is a Jew, and *Gerim* have always been a part of our *mesora*. This time is as good as any to not only perform a tremendous *mitzvah* in making *Gerim* [and facilitating the Noahide Path], but to take part in the early days of the Messiah. At the very least, assuming we are not in the actual days of the Messiah, we are witnessing a *Ger* return that rivals similar events in our past, namely Purim. Our ancestors have always shown us the art of making *Gerim*, going back to the *Gerim* that were made by Abraham and Sarah. One can only wonder if this has happened with Kla'l Yisrael's visible return to Zion of our time.

In conclusion, we stand before two *shitot*: one is Noahide [*lefi pshuto*], that excludes *Ger Toshav,* and the other one is *Toras Emes,* that includes both Noahides and *Ger Toshav*. This *shita* is brought down by the Rambam, as explained by the Rebbe [and others]. The other well-intentioned *shita* is a modern invention, aimed at keeping Gentiles safely at bay until a Messiah comes and rescues. Although the situation at hand appears to be

Messianic in nature, in reality it is not. It is a *halachic* matter, and one that has been preserved in *halacha* for over 2,000 years. While changing the *halacha* may seem like the safe bet, it is wrong, and delays the *geulah*. Quite the contrary, it should go without saying that keeping and promoting the true *halacha* will only hasten the true redemption, may it be quickly hastened in our days!

Afterword

~~

The Rebbe on B'nai Noah and learning Torah, based on Likutei Sichos

The Lubavitcher Rebbe says that we have an obligation of the highest order to help the *B'nai Noah* fulfill their *Mitzvot* through Talmud Torah.[58] The Rebbe quotes the Rambam[59] concerning the role of *Klal Yisrael* that will take place in the Days of the Messiah. It is known that the Rebbe said repeatedly that *Am Yisrael* has entered into these exciting times, and now more than ever, the fruit of the Rebbe's [Noahide] work is clearly visible and has become a part of today's Judaism at large [in many capacities]. The non-Jews have fulfilled their destiny and are returning to our Holy Torah with the exact prescription about which our Oral Torah has spoken for thousands of years. They have accepted their place in the Oral Torah and are acting according to strict *halacha*.

The Torah contains a crystal-clear tradition that outlines the *Kosher* path for a Torah non-Jew to abide by. The Rebbe highlights this path by showing its relationship to the coming of

---

[58] *Likutei Sichos* vol. 27 pp. 246-7; see footnotes.

[59] *Hilchot Melachim* Ch. 11.

the Messiah and the Messianic age, and the nature of our obligatory cooperation with the invigorated righteous gentile who has properly rejected his religion, turned away from idols, and has accepted the Oral Torah [through his relationship with the Seven Laws] of Sinai. This is called a rejection of *Shituf*, and according to the Rambam [as quoted by the Rebbe] this is the only accepted way a gentile can be regarded as a true *Ben Noah*. The Rebbe[60] calls this 'Seven Laws *Ger Toshav*,' as they have chosen to make a *shayachess* to *Dinei Yisrael* and *Dinei Torah* [*Dat HaEmes*]. All *halachic* authorities[61] recognize this distinction and hold that to further use such a *Ben Noah* as a 'Shabbos Goy' carries with it a prohibition weighted as a *Dorisa*. This *Ben Noah* [even of today] through his *shayachess* to *Dinei Torah* is synonymously attached to *Din Ger Toshav* in some matters. Though he be a *Ben Noah*, he also carries a responsibility to himself and to *Klal Yisrael* as a partial *Ger Toshav* [in some matters]. A full *Ger Toshav* only exists in a time of Jubilee. See above, *Ode Yisrael Yosef Beni Chai*, by Rav Ahron Soloveichik, where the numerous distinctions and concepts are laid out with clarity and diligence. The Rebbe's *sicha* vol. 31 also lays out the exact same subject matter, with a particular interest of clarifying the *Ger Toshav* of today concerning *Hilchot Shabbos* based on *Krisos* 9a. The *Ger Toshav* is commanded to not be a *Shabbos Goy*, while being commanded to not totally refrain from performing *Melacha*.

---

[60] *Likutei Sichos* vol. 31 *Parashas Mishpatim.*

[61] *Shulchan Aruch* 304; *Krisos* 9a.

The Rebbe states that the Nations returning to our Holy Faith are accepting their role as prescribed by the Torah of Moses; this is a *'Chiddush Gadol'* and he bases this on a quote from the Rambam, who refers to the Prophet Isaiah who intimates that in the Days of the Messiah, and leading up to it, the 'Entire World' will be filled with Knowing God. The Rebbe explains that the Rambam's words 'Entire World' should be taken quite literally as the 'Entire World' - Jew and Gentile - *Ben Noah*. As source material to further elucidate the words of the Rambam, the Rebbe draws from classic Torah sources in his *Likutei Sichos* in order to explain and outline the obligations of the *B'nai Noah* in the Torah and for Jews concerning their role in facilitating the return of *B'nai Noah* to Torah, according to *halacha* and mainstream Judaism [*Dinei Ger Toshav*]. The Rebbe clearly states that this is a part of the process of the complete redemption and in revealing the Torah of our Righteous Messiah.

The Rebbe explains the Rambam's Torah that in this process the Gentiles will return to our Faith, The True Faith, and to the Torah on their own. This is called *'Gerim Grurim,'*[62] and Rashi explains why these returnees are called *'Ger'* or *'Gerim,'* which is

---

[62] *Avodah Zara* 24a.

consistent with *Chazal* and the entire *Mesora*; they *Megair* themselves and at a time when Jews are not '*Mekablin*' *Gerim*.[63]

The only way that this can be achieved and be perceived as *Kosher* is if the Nations in their return do so in accordance of the Seven Laws *B'nai Noah* / Seven Laws *Ger Toshav*.[64] Once they enter into the True Faith, according to *halacha*, the *halachic* system of the *Mesora* employs a strict system that associates properly to the Torah observant gentile. Some of the Torah governed relationships are: wine, interest, *kashrut*, Shabbos, Holidays, *middos*, Tanach History, precedent, *halacha*, terminology, *hashkafa*, *kabbalah*, *chassidus*, *darkei shalom*, *derech eretz*, charity, Temple protocol, matters of impurity, understanding of text and commentary, *mitzvot*, nature of transgression [stumbling block before the blind], Tanach content [Tehillim], etc. All of the above require knowledge of Gentiles in Torah and/or working with Gentiles in a Torah capacity.

The Rebbe finalizes his vision by quoting from the Meiri[65] who shows that the Torah inspired *Ben Noah* who learns Torah is compared to the *Kohen Gadol*, to which the Rebbe states that this

---

[63] Not a full conversion; in *halacha* it is called *Ktzat Geirus - Ger Toshav*; see Rashba where he states all language 'Ger' and 'Giur' can be either *Ger Gamur* or *Ktzat Geirus* and only Torah context reveals the true meaning.

[64] Rambam *Hilchot Melachim* ch. 8:10-11.

[65] *Sanhedrin* 59a.

means he wears a type of Priestly Crown – in that he is to make an occupation of *Mitzvas* Talmud Torah in the Seven Laws [*Ger Toshav*]. The Rebbe points out that this is only made possible through the Jew who teaches the *B'nai Noah* Torah – and whom the Rambam calls 'A Sage of Israel' when in this capacity. The two of them fulfill the Knowing of God and help usher in the Messianic Era. The Jew will then appropriately wear the higher crown, the Crown of Torah. These roles cannot be reversed and are designed to work in this way, the way that clarified by the Rambam, the Rebbe explains. The Jew who properly wears the Crown of Torah will draw from the Sages of Israel and help usher in the complete redemption and the Torah of the Messiah, while being a *kosher* Holy Torah Light to Nations, as it says, the Nations will recognize the Jewish Nation's greatness only through their Torah Wisdom.[66]

The Torah carries a tradition from the Sages that the Gentiles are destined to leave idolatry, even *Shituf*, and will embrace the Sinai Code with enough fervor that they will embrace the True Faith and keep the Seven Laws according to Sinai, along with a commitment to their study through the Torah of Moses in the prescribed way.[67] This is the meaning of 'A *Nochri* who learns Torah is like a *Kohen Gadol.*' There is a *girsa* in *Midrash Tanchuma* that is the basis of this concept in *halacha*, and in place of '*Nochri*'

---

[66] Gra in *Midrash Shlomo.*

[67] *Meiri Sanhedrin* 59a.

employs the appropriate term 'Ger' ... 'who learns Torah is like the Kohen Gadol.'

To this there are only two questions that anyone ever asks: 'A *goy* who learns Torah is *chayav misa*,'[68] and therefore 'Does a Jew have any responsibilities toward Gentiles/Gentile neighbors?'[69] The Rebbe answers these questions by identifying the *'Gerim Grurim'* as the subject matter of the Rambam[70] and describes the process as properly teaching/learning about Seven Laws [*Ger Toshav*] and removes all doubt by illustrating how this is the process of the complete redemption, which he calls a *'Chiddush Gadol.'*

In conclusion, the Rebbe has given us the clear path that Jews should walk on through the *Mesora*, namely the Talmud and *Rishonim*, like the Ran, Meiri, and Rambam, as well as highlighting the path that the Gentiles will walk on. By adhering to his words, we strengthen our Holy Torah and take part in the Messianic Era, hastening it in the days that lead up to the complete redemption.

The only lingering question that both Jew and Gentile both struggle with, is the burning question of where there is a

---

[68] Rambam *Hilchot Melachim* 10:9; not to be confused with the *Ben Noah*, who can do *Mitzvot* even according to their *Halacha* - ibid. 10:10.

[69] See above, *Ode Yisrael Yosef Beni Chai*, which details this latter point exclusively.

[70] *Hilchot Melachim* Ch. 11.

precedent in Torah of the truly Righteous Gentile. This basic concept is usually shrouded by poor English translations that have grown accustomed to translating 'Ger' as 'convert,' when in truth convert is only one type of 'Ger.' The Torah is filled with many non-convert 'Gerim,' and this is the 'Ger/Gerim' spoken about at great length throughout the entire Mesora. We have examples like Antoninus, Jethro, Rachav, the Rechabites and Kenites, and Naaman, to name a few. This type of Torah character is promised to happen again; it is what the Rambam is describing as the Messianic process; and we are seeing it begin in our times. The Rebbe saw it and brought it out, and we are witnessing an even stronger exodus of Gentiles leaving their fallen faith and returning to the True Faith[71] and in accordance with *halacha* and *Torat Moshe*.

Even if it is 'one from a city and two from a family,' we are witnessing and participating in a process that the Rebbe calls a 'Chiddush Gadol,' and the Torah has contained this wisdom from Sinai, anticipating the fateful time when the Gentiles would return as *Gerim Grurim*, *B'nai Noah* who wish to keep the Seven Laws *Ger Toshav* in order to become 'Nilveh Ger' to Israel.[72]

We are in exciting times, and this is not disputed. It is a 'Chiddush Gadol' – a time to be a Light to Nations, and with that comes the

---

[71] *Likutei Sichos* vol. 23 pp. 41,179,195

[72] Isaiah 14:1 & 56:3

Crown of Torah and the Wisdom to Know God. As the Rambam points out, and the Rebbe clarifies, it is our job as the Jewish People to bring Knowledge of God to the entire world, and this will elevate *B'nai Noah* into the best *Gerei Toshavim* that they can be. They will be allowed to perform their Seven *Mitzvot* in such a way that they can occupy themselves with the Torah study embedded into the Seven Laws of *Ger Toshav*. What has been kept as a *Chiddush Gadol* will become a Light to Nations, and what the Rebbe has been teaching has come to fruition.

Appendix[73]

[73] The repetition in terms is for the purpose of clarity and reiteration. Many of the terms carry multiple connotations and change through context. The subtle nuances of many of the key terms mandate reiteration for the sake of clarity and comprehension.

Ger FAQ
(Ikkar Klalim)

1. *Ger Toshav*, as an official status, does not exist until the Jubilee Year.[74]

2. Someone today can be considered <u>like</u> a *Ger Toshav* (*k'ger toshav*), but is still not a *Ger Toshav*. To accomplish being considered <u>like</u> a *Ger Toshav*, is the subject matter of deep scholarship.[75]

3. A Jew may not marry a *Ger Toshav*; all intermarriage is forbidden and will never be allowed, even in the Messianic age. The Jewish People have accepted to not engage in this practice, and should a non-Jew wish to marry a Jewish person under *Kosher* circumstances, a proper *halachic* conversion would be mandatory. A proper conversion is strictly for the

---

[74] *Ger* [*Toshav*] is not a movement. The purpose of this work is to create a Torah and *halachic* awareness of the *Ger* [*Toshav*] *sugia*, thereby fascilitating the working relationships between Jews and non-Jews as has been done on a generation by generation basis. The *Ger Toshav sugia* has been the hallmark of maintaining [Torah] peace in the world, and making this content known in this generation is imperative.

[75] Rabbi Ahron Soloveichik wrote extensively on this subject matter. See *Ode Yisrael Yosef Beni Chai*, above.

sake of Heaven, to become a part of the Jewish People and a Torah observant Jew.

4.   A *Ger Toshav* can observe Shabbos in his/her own way, but does not keep Shabbos like a Jew. He is obligated to perform *Melacha*.[76]

5.   A person considered <u>like</u> a *Ger Toshav*, i.e. a non-idolater, has renounced all previous religion. In other words, he is no longer Christian, Muslim, etc. He is also not Jewish; however, he accepts his role in observing *mitzvot* according to Jewish Faith. Jewish Faith is complete in its doctrines of how to relate to a pious person from among the Nations.

6.   A *Ger Toshav* is not allowed to serve as a *Shabbos goy*.[77] Part of their commitment to God is by not doing *Melacha* for a Jew; they respectfully decline. For full comprehension of this law, see *Hilchot Shabbos*; particularly the laws of when one is dangerously ill.

7.   The Torah mentions *Ger* nearly 100 times, and hardly ever does the term exclusively come to imply a convert to Judaism. Most of the times the term can apply

---

[76] See *Krisos* 9a for the prescribed manner to which this is done.

[77] See *Mishneh Breura O.C.* 304 for full *halachic* application of *Ger Toshav* concerning *Hilchot Shabbos*; also see *Likutei Sichos* Vol. 31 *Parashas Mishpatim* for the full view of *Ger Toshav* in *Hilchot Shabbos b'zman hazeh*.

simultaneously to a Jewish convert *Ger* and a non-convert *Ger*. This is called *ribui*, inclusion. The opposite is called *miyut*, exclusion. The Torah commentaries are complete with knowledge of when to read '*Ger*' as a *ribui* or *miyut*.

8. There are levels of *Ger Toshav* that exist for all of time. A few examples are:

- A Jew has a commandment to offer *neveilah* freely to the *Ger Toshav,* as opposed to selling it to the idolater.

- A non-idolater, a *Ger Toshav*, may be left alone with Jewish wine in the home of a Jew.

- A non-idolater, *Ger Toshav* is not to be a *Shabbos goy*.

Jubilee doesn't factor into either scenario; this status exists at all times. This is called an incomplete *Ger Toshav*, i.e. is connected to the *din* of *Ger Toshav*, as opposed to the *Ger Toshav* with official *halachic* status after the Jubilee. [78]

Din shel Ger Toshav [*k'tzat inyanim*]: A non-Jew who keeps the Seven Laws of Noah is considered as having the '*din shel Ger Toshav*' [*k'tzat inyanim*] when a Torah Law applicable is applicable to him. For example, he is forbidden to act as a *Shabbos goy* because he carries '*din shel Ger Toshav.*'

---

[78] For further analysis between the status of full *Ger Toshav* at the time of Jubilee and *Ger Toshav* non-Jubilee, effective at all times, see above R. Soloveichik '*Ode Yisrael Yosef Beni Chai.*'

9. The Torah states many times that in the End of Days, non-Jews will return to God by their own desires, in a time when the Jewish People aren't prepared to receive them.[79] These returnees are called *Gerim Grurim*,[80] and this is one reason why these people are called '*Gerim*' in short. The Torah refers to them and this dynamic as such in those terms. However, for the purposes of clarity we will attempt to use the term *Ger Toshav* in all such cases.

10. The Rambam employs two terms for the *kosher* righteous gentile: *Ger Toshav* and 'From the *Chasidei Umot HaOlam*.'[81]

The term '*Chasidei Umot HaOlam*' implies their commitment to carefully fulfilling the Seven Laws and, therefore, their worthiness to merit a portion in the World to Come.

The term *Ger Toshav* implies that they have removed their foreskin spiritually, enough to merit this level, referring to their internal *kavanah*.

---

[79] *Avodah Zara* 24a, see Rashi.

[80] Self-returning, as Rashi states, 'They cause themselves to become *Gerim* even though we don't accept them.' The *Gemara* says the *Gerim Grurim* are the fulfillment of Zephaniah 3:9: 'I will change the nations [to speak] a pure language, so that they will proclaim the Name of Hashem, to worship Him with united resolve.'

[81] *Hilchot Melachim* 8:10-11.

The Rambam holds that by keeping the Seven Laws of Noah, with proper intent, and with proper acceptance [*kabbalah*], they have done the equivalent of a pre-requisite removal of their foreskin. There are two levels of this spiritual circumcision. The higher level is in accordance with Jewish standards, and will culminate as a *halachic* Jewish conversion. The lower level is not *halachic* (neither spiritually nor physically) and only serves to remove the label of 'uncircumcised.' This second level of spiritual circumcision, according to the Rambam, does not make the person a Jew in any way, but it does warrant certain benefits, such as meriting the World to Come, etc.

11. Rejection of *Shituf* is one of the core distinctions between a non-Jew who keeps the Seven Laws of Noah and the *Ger Toshav*. *Shituf* means the belief that Hashem shares His power with some other entity or partner. Examples of *shituf* are when a yogi, a master or a prophetic teacher becomes viewed as a god or in some way interchangeable with God. Noahides are only commanded to reject idolatry, but not to proactively believe in God. A *Ger Toshav* proactively believes in God, which through proper *kabbalah* is a clear *halachic* display of rejecting *Shituf*.

Shituf is permitted for Noahides. As long as a Noahide has not formally rejected *shituf,* the presumption is that he is still not believing in the God of Israel. Although it is permitted, it encouraged to reject *shituf* and is praiseworthy. A Jew who identifies a non-Jew who has naturally come to reject *shituf* has an incumbent obligation to associate with the non-Jew as someone considered to be <u>like</u> a *Ger Toshav*.

12. The concept of "*kabbalah*" means to officially accept this new status in front of a *Bet din*. There are two levels of *kabbalah/Bet din* in declaring *Ger Toshav*, one which applies only after the Jubilee is reestablished, and one which applies at all times, including today:

- At the time of Jubilee. Once the Jubilee is reestablished the action of acceptance (*Kabbalah/Bet din*) confers an actual *halachic Ger Toshav*, or resident alien status. This acceptance ensures that the subject is, at minimum, not an idolater, and makes him/her eligible to live in the Land of Israel. When there is no Jubilee, this is impossible to achieve, and thus certain benefits cannot come into play until this level of *Bet din* is operative.

- Prior to the time of Jubilee. A secondary *Bet din* (three Jewish men, not necessarily Torah scholars) can be set up at any time and in any place. It grants *Ger Toshav* status on a lesser level; it is an inferior *kabbalah* to that of one in a time of Jubilee and has spiritual, non-*halachic* status, although it does change our relationship with the *Ger Toshav* within the realm of *halacha*. This secondary, present-time level of *kabbalah* requires the *Ger Toshav* to officially renounce idolatry, including *shituf*, and it serves to move them from the realm of *acum* to someone who has a level of relationship with the Jewish People and the Jewish mission. It also serves to elevate the *Ger Toshav* to a standing of Sinai, i.e. to a level where he can receive reward for performing the Seven Laws of Noah as one who is 'commanded and does.' This is also called *Ger Toshav*, and it should not be confused with *Ger Toshav* status [to live in the Land of Israel] which can only happen in a time of Jubilee.

13. An incomplete *Ger Toshav* (the non-Jubilee level of present-time *kabbalah*) is called a Ben Noah in certain places.[82] The term Ben Noah in *mesora* can imply *Ger Toshav, Chasid Umot HaOlam, Ben Noah kosher/gamor,* or goy/*acum*; to understand this thoroughly requires deep study. The Rambam states that a Ben Noah[83] can perform any commandment in the Torah for the sake of receiving reward. However, they will be performing on the level of one who is 'not commanded and does.' To avoid confusion, *poskim* call the Ben Noah, who is synonymous with the incomplete *Ger Toshav,* either a *Ben Noah kosher* or *Ben Noah gamor.*

---

[82] Rambam, *Hilchot Melachim* 10:10

[83] See *Ode Yisrael Yosef Beni Chai,* above, which clarifies that the Ben Noah of Rambam *Hilchot Melachim* 10:10 is synonymous with the incomplete *Ger Toshav.*

For context, a Jew is always considered as being 'commanded and does' when any of the 613 commandments are performed. A *Ger Toshav* [one with *kabbalah*] has the status of 'commanded and does' over the Seven Laws of Noah. Again, this status is not available at this time, as the Jubilee is not yet in force.

14. Any *Ger Toshav* is not only permitted to learn Torah, but is praised for his doing so. (The nuances for permissible Torah learning for the non-Jew are subtle and complex, and this requires deep analysis.) In *Baba Kama* 38a it says that 'A *Ger* who learns Torah is considered like a High Priest.' (This concept is explained by the Lubavitcher Rebbe). In contrast, a non-Jew who learns certain parts of Torah without *kabbalah* comes under the status of 'a *goy* who learns Torah is liable for the death penalty.' These matters require deep introspection to fully understand in all of their *halachic* nuances.

In either case, a Ben Noah has an inherent obligation of Talmud Torah concerning his/her own Torah obligations, i.e. the Seven Laws of Noah. Any other Torah study must be in connection with an intention of performing a permissible deed. The Torah study is an aide in performing the deed. These laws need looking into for practical application, for 'a *goy* who learns Torah is liable for the death penalty,' and a *Ger Toshav* who learns Torah is 'like a High Priest'; and there is no contradiction. The spiritual principle here, which is reflected in the *halacha*, is that the desire and commitment of the *Ger Toshav* to come close to and serve Hashem entitles him/her to a completely different relationship with the Torah.

15. *Ger* does not literally mean 'convert.' Convert is only one type of *Ger*. The terms: *Ger, Ger Toshav, Ger Tzedek*, etc. each carry multiple meanings; in order to correctly understand these, and their relevance/usage in our times, scholarship of Rabbinic writings and mastery of the Oral Torah (*Rishonim*, in particular) on this subject is mandatory.

    To illustrate the complexity of meaning, an *Eved Canaani*, who is circumcised and has gone to *mikvah* is considered a *Ger Tzedek*, but he is neither a Jew nor a convert. An *Eved Canaani*, who is not circumcised, is considered a *Ger Toshav* if he accepts the Seven Laws of Noah, as he is required to do to be the servant of a Jew. This level of *Ger Toshav* is not a *Chasid Umot HaOlam*, i.e. he is not righteous for having become a slave, yet the same term is used [*Ger Toshav*] in both instances. The Brisker Rav calls this '*tzvei dinim*' – two laws that derive from one term/concept.

16. There is a commandment to Love the *Ger*. It is not always clear if the *Ger Toshav* is included in this precept. All rule that even if the *Ger Toshav* is not included, if it only refers to a *Ger Tzedek* [convert or non-convert, i.e. a slave or one who stops

just short of conversion[84]], the commandment, at the very least, comes to teach ethics about how to treat strangers who wish sincerely to approach us as friends. These strangers, regardless of *halachic* status, are called *Gerim*. They are real people, and they exist eternally. We are encouraged to recognize them and to treat them well. They are *Gerim*.

17. Mastery of the meaning-laden terminology [*ikkarim*] is essential, for only through mastery of the terminology can one ascertain which type/level of *Ger* [*Toshav*] is being spoken of in any specific source. Terminology is not empty; on the contrary, each term is full of background meaning, which any scholar in the topic will understand without its being explained.

    For example, the Rambam differentiates between the *Ger Toshav* status that comes from Jubilee vs. the status of *Chasid* (*Chasidei Umot HaOlam*) – one is related to the slave while the other is righteous, having chosen to this higher relationship of his own free will. He also distinguishes between the *goy* and the Ben Noah, and Ben Noah itself has multiple meanings which depend upon context.

    Please note: the entire Oral Torah works along these lines, and most of the time the *Rishonim* 'copy and paste' their source work from *Chazal*. To quote King Solomon: 'The words

---

[84] *Mishnah Breura* 304.

of the sages come in riddles.' Case in point: 'a *goy* who learns Torah is liable for the death penalty' is more of a riddle than a literal decree. It is a *mashel*, and the *nimshal* needs to be sought out and understood. Commentaries are plentiful, and every Torah scholar knows that one cannot rely on the literal interpretation. In fact, this complex system of learning the *ikkarim*, decoding the sources and bringing out an accurate and multi-layered understanding, is the core function for which the Oral Torah was written.

18. It is fundamental to this entire subject to understand that a non-Jew can elevate out of an uncircumcised state, and without the need to convert; it goes without saying that only one who converts can literally become part of the Jewish People. This non-conversion elevation process is referred to as *Ger* in the written Torah (*Ger* can refer to both non-convert and convert), and it is called *Ger Toshav* in the Oral Torah. Once a non-Jew has rejected *shituf*, he/she is no longer considered as one of the nations; this act, when sincere, makes him/her a *Ger Toshav* (non-Jew).

19. An Yishmaelite is considered a *bedieved Ger Toshav*, and can be used for rabbinic permissions of *Ger Toshav*, e.g. the State of Israel's *Heter Mechira*.

Nevertheless, a Yishmaelite is still considered an *acum* (*goy*), does not have a complete circumcision, i.e., is still considered as having a foreskin, and does not enjoy any of the higher liberties of the righteous non-Jew, who has consciously chosen to not serve idols, i.e. a *Chasid* of the nations. This Yishmaelite is used in a strictly *bedieved* way, whereas the *Ger Toshav* of our times is not as *bedieved* in these situations. For example, if a Jew was standing before a *nochri*, an Yishmaelite, and a Noahide in terms of giving *neveilah*, the proper manner is to give the *neveilah* to the Noahide and to sell it to the *nochri* and the Yishmaelite.

This is a nuanced situation in our times, and it is important to understand that no matter how sincerely a non-Jew keeps the Seven Laws with *kabbalah*, it is only at a time of Jubilee that a *Ger Toshav* status will be employed on a *lechatchila* basis.

20. It is crucial to understand that although these matters are immensely important and relevant in these times, historically, matters of *Ger*[*im*] have been dangerous, for the Talmud warns, 'harsh like thorns are *Gerim* upon Israel.' This is a *halachic* fact. However, in spite of the inherent danger, it is a *mitzvah* to making *Gerim*.[85]

In our times the *Ger Toshav* partners with the Jewish mission, lives outside the Land of Israel, and although he is categorically not Jewish, has a *halachic* connection with the Jewish People. It is important to specify that even in the times

---

[85] See *The Mitzvah to Make Gerim.*

of the Jubilee the *Ger Toshav* will not belong to the Holy House of Israel, but rather to the fourth, non-holy House.[86] An actual *halachic* convert to Judaism, in contrast, becomes a full Jew, enters into the third Holy House of Israel (*Yisrael*), and has the right and obligation to marry another Jew. Likewise, his/her children will be Jewish. This conversion is considered *lechatchila* when their motivation is to be a Jew, to be a full part of the Jewish People and produce Jewish offspring. If their intention is merely to marry Jewish, this is ill-advised, and is considered *bedieved*. (This fourth, non-holy house is hinted at spiritually in Psalm 135:20. Where it says: 'those who fear Hashem,' the commentators identify the God-fearers as *Gerim/Chassidei Umot Haolam*. Rabbi Yitzchak Ginsburgh likens this to the four-headed *shin*.)

In contrast to the *halachic* convert, a *Ger Toshav* does not seek to be a native Jew, but seeks to live and serve God through the holy principles of Judaism and Torah, for example to reject *shituf*.

21. The core foundational principle is this: A non-Jew can serve God in a *kosher* and holy way as a *Ger Toshav*, including the rejection of *shituf*, even before the Jubilee. He does not need to convert in order to do so, and if he/she is not 100% certain

---

[86] See: http://getsoulstrong.blogspot.co.il/2017/02/what-is-israels-4th-house.html

about, and committed to, full conversion, this should not be pushed. On the contrary, conversion which is not fully grounded and committed causes problems, not only for the convert, but for all of Israel. Instead, the Torah offers this sincere non-Jew the option of becoming a *Ger Toshav*.

22. *Ger Toshav* is not limited to a resident alien living in the Land of Israel, and the word *Toshav* does not always mean 'resident.' *Ger Toshav* is not mentioned anywhere in the written Torah [nor is *Ger Tzedek*]; *Ger* is, and therefore the Oral Torah comes to explain the understandings of context and connotation that are absolutely required to understand the Law.

Toshav is a rabbinic term that expresses that one is deemed *kosher* enough to live in Israel, not that he is actually living in Israel. [The Rambam states the term *Toshav* means he is permitted, *Issurei Biah* 14:7. This is the same *Ger Toshav* of *Hilchot Melachim* 8, 10, 11, i.e. not a *Ger Toshav* Jubilee, *Issurei Biah* 14:8,9.[87]] *Toshav* is effectively a *hechsher*: a sign of being *kosher*. A *Ger Toshav* is one who has taken *kabbalah* to be careful with the Seven *Mitzvot*, such that one can be sure that there is no longer a hint of idolatry, even *shituf*.

---

[87] See the *Psak* of the Lubavitcher Rebbe.

23. As long as there is still no Jubilee, we cannot produce a *Bet din* that is authorized to confer this level. However, we can perform a lesser *Bet din/kabbalah* and create a *Ger Toshav* for lesser observance, all in the spirit of being "fit" to live in the Land, i.e., carrying the same requirements for level of commitment and observance without the actual *halachic* status. Since the sanctity of the *kabbalah* is lesser in a non-Jubilee time, the sanctity of the *Ger Toshav* that is produced is of a lesser state. Today for instance, one can be a *Ger Toshav*, but cannot be deemed actually *kosher* to live in the Land of Israel. Such a person can, however, be left alone with Jewish wine as a *Ger Toshav*, even without taking *kabbalah*, i.e. even a Yishmaelite level *Ger Toshav*. The difference is that in Jubilee we are certain that they aren't idolaters, while today we strongly believe that they are not idolaters. The difference illustrated by their relationship with Jewish wine is one of a rabbinic decree vs. a scriptural one. There is room to be lenient when the prohibition is rabbinic as opposed to when the prohibition is scriptural and the consequences are infinitely more severe. The examples are many, and again, scholarship is of the essence.[88]

24. A *Ger Toshav* may not participate in any specifically Jewish ritual or service that requires one to be a member of the Jewish People, e.g. *aliyot, minyan, zimun, birkat kohanim*, etc.

---

[88] See Rabbi Ahron Soloveichik's '*Ode Yisrael Yosef Beni Chai.*'

Concerning a *Ger Toshav* and the performance of *mitzvot* of *kedusha* and *tahara*, see Radvaz on Rambam, *Hilchot Melachim* 10:10.

25. Much of the unfortunate controversy and confusion that we experience today around this very important issue has come from the fact that *Ger* has come to be routinely translated as 'convert.' We need look no further than *Parshas Reeh*, 14:21, where it states: "Give the *neveilah* to the *Ger in your gates.*"

It is unmistakably obvious that we do not give *neveilah* to a convert. From this alone it is clear that *Ger* does not always mean convert. It is my hope that this will serve as a *Binyan Av* that whenever one comes across the word *Ger*, whether it be in *halacha*, *chassidus*, *kabbalah*, *midrash*, Talmud, *siddur*, *Tanach*, *Rishonim*, *Achronim*, or any other source, the reader will become curious enough to look beyond the English translation in front of him and discern the correct usage and meaning of the word in accordance with the sources.

In almost every case, the meaning, once one is resolved to understand it correctly, will require at least minimal research into the relevant sources to make this understanding clear.

26. The Jew is not commanded to return *Gerim* to the Torah the same way he has an obligation to return *baalei teshuva* to the Torah. Nonetheless, the Lubavitcher Rebbe states that it is a

tremendous *mitzvah* to make *Gerim*, when the opportunity presents itself. In other words, the *mitzvah* of making *gerim* is a *reshut* rather than a *chovah*.

27. The righteous non-Jew of the *Chumash* is called *Ger*. The Biblical *Ger* is found in the Talmud on two levels: *Ger Tzedek*[89] and *Ger Toshav*.[90] The Jewish People are familiar with *Ger Tzedek*, referring to converts, simply as '*Ger*.' It is just as appropriate to link *Ger Toshav*[91] back to *Ger* , as it is written in the *Chumash*.[92] *Ger*, as it is written in this way for the righteous non-Jew, is synonomous with '*Ger in your gates*.'[93] The following examples shed light on the advantages of referring to righteous non-Jews as *Gerim*: [94]   a *Ger who learns Torah*, a *Ger* who rejects *shituf*, an *acum* who becomes *Ger* , the *mitzvah* to love the *Ger*, **gerim** *grurim*, a *Ger* who takes *kabbalah*, forty-six mentions of 'don't taunt the *Ger* ,' the *mitzvot* regarding the '*Ger in your gates*,' and the *nilvah Ger*. *Ger*, the dimunitive of '*Ger Toshav*,' is not only *halachically* correct, it is also found throughout sources of *Machshava* and

---

[89] Convert for the sake of taking on *mitzvot*.

[90] *Avodah Zara* 64b.

[91] Rambam *Hilchot* Melachim 8:10-11.

[92] *Ger* has two meanings, i.e., *tzvei dinim*.

[93] Ramban *Shemot* 20:10.

[94] The *Ger Toshav* of today is not a particial conversion, and there is no suspicion of creating a new religion.

Agadata.[95] *Ger Toshav* is a *sugia* that spans the entire Torah, and studying it is an eyeopener of the various designations of non-Jews. The laws pertinent to them are often not known, or distorted.[96] It is unfortunate that there are *hashkafos* that stand against this holy subject matter[97] for it distorts and inhibits the Jewish Mission in the world to be a Light unto the Nations. The Torah[98] is clear as to who and what the *Ger*[99] is and makes heavy use of this vernacular in all aspects of Torah. *Ger* in its diminutive is not limited to convert/*Ger Tzedek,* as it equally pertains to *Ger Toshav.*[100] When the Rambam speaks about *Ger Toshav,*[101] who rejects *shituf* and is careful to keep the Seven Laws of Noah, he is to be considered as being 'from

---

[95] For example: *Pesachim* 87b, *Tehillim* Rashi 135:20, *Likutei Moharan* 1:17:4, and many others throughout the *Mesora.*

[96] Rabbi Leff's *haskama,* pg 17.

[97] 'Much of the attitudes of our community concerning this subject was, and is, acquired only through osmosis of the historical experiences of our community rather than through the actual study of the texts of the Oral Tradition.' Rabbi Moshe Soloveichek's *haskama,* pg 18.

[98] Oral and written Torah.

[99] Righteous non-Jew.

[100] Most appropriately, '*Ger in your gates.*' *Ger* is a diminutive of both *Ger Toshav* and '*ger in your gates.*' *Ger Toshav* is not always synonomous with '*Ger in your gates.*' *Ger Toshav* is limited to *halachic* discussions, while '**Ger** *in your gates*' exists *halachically,* philosophically, and is the language of the relevant *mitzvot* concerning *Gerim* and the prophetic sayings that involve the *nilvah Ger.*

[101] *Hilchot Melachim* 8:10-11.

the Pious of the Nations.' Rabbi Nachum Eliezer Rabinovitch teaches that these *B'nai Noah* are called *Chasidim*. It would seem to me that one can call a *Ben Noah Gamor* like this a *Ger Chasid*, without losing any integrity from the words of the Rambam.

28. *Tikun Olam* falls upon the Jewish People. One aspect of *Tikun Olam* is making *Gerim*, and in turn, *Ger im* help the Jewish People in *Tikun Olam*. But that does not change the fact that the ultimate responsibility for this task belongs to the Jewish People. Historically, the presence of the *Gerim* is a sign that the Jewish People are engaging in their special mission to be a Light to the Nations. This happened in the days of the Patriarchs, the Exodus from Egypt, the days of David and Solomon, the days of Purim, and B"H, in the days that we are in now – the Footsteps of Moshiach.

Elucidation of Terms

1. *Acum*: acronym denoting common 'idolater.' There are various degrees of idolatry that come under the term '*acum*,' ranging from a purely wicked '*acum*' to a level of *acum* that a Jew can interact with under Torah Law. Its ultimate meaning is contingent upon its usage in each specific text.

2. *Am Yisrael*: The Jewish People proper, denoting the Nation of Israel/Jewish People who are comprised of Cohanim, Leviim, Israelites, and Israelite Converts.

3. *Apikorsim*: Israelites who reject the rabbinic tradition of Oral Torah.

4. *Ben Noah*: A term that has become synonymous with the label 'Noahide.' It specifically represents the three sons of Noah and their offspring, and to the revelation of Torah Law delivered to Noah. In the Talmud, its meaning can range anywhere from a general term for a gentile, to a person who keeps the Seven Laws of Noah, to all of humanity, its meaning depending on the context in each specific text.

5. *Ben Noah Gamor*: A complete *Ben Noah*. An elevated status of a gentile, who keeps the Seven Laws of Noah in a time when the Jubilee Year is in operation, and has accepted them in a rabbinic court of law. A synonymous term may refer to this as '*Ben Noah Kosher*.'

6. *Darchei Shalom*: A Torah Law that mandates the pursuit of peace for a higher religious 'good.' In certain situations. The Torah instructs the preservation of peace

with non-Jews even though the situation may not warrant it.

7. *Din shel Ger Toshav* [*k'tzat inyanim*]: A non-Jew who keeps the Seven Laws of Noah is considered as having the *'din shel Ger Toshav'* [*k'tzat inyanim*] when a Torah Law applicable is applicable to him. For example, he is forbidden to act as a *Shabbos goy* because he carries *'din shel Ger Toshav.'*

8. *Ger Toshav*: A status given to a non-Jew who formally keeps the Seven Laws of Noah. This designation distinguishes him from an *acum*.

9. *Ger Toshav Gamor*: A full status granted to an observant gentile through a specific Jewish court in a time period when Torah Law is fully observable, i.e. in a Jubilee Time Period.

10. *Goyim*: non-Jews, non-*Ger Toshav*. Synonymous with gentile, [some] *Ben Noah*, [some] Noahides, *acum*, *nochri*. There are other times when '*goyim*' can imply 'idolatrous.'

11. *Ha-megushim*: people who physicalize things and deny the spirituality of the Torah.

12. *Chasidei Umot Ha-Olam*: A gentile who either identifies himself as a 'lover of Israel,' or strives to observe the Seven Laws of Noah, or functions appropriately as a *Ger Toshav*. In a more literal sense, these are the people who are elevated in righteousness out of the category of being 'of the nations,' to become 'quasi-Gentiles.'

13. Jubilee Year: A 50th Year Sabbatical in the Land of Israel. When in force full *Ger Toshav* status is available, thus enabling complete opportunity for appropriate Torah Law observance for the *Ger Toshav* who is now *'Gamor.'*

14. *Kofrim*: people who deny the existence of God or the Godliness of the Torah.

15. *Lo maalim v'lo moridim*: Literally 'do not bring them up and do not bring them down,' meaning do not help them and do not hurt them. This is an informal law conferred upon non-Jews when higher understanding of their character has yet to be established.

16. *Lo Tichanem* (Deut. 7:2): 'Do not be gracious to them,' a Torah Law designed for a Jew to not mingle with an idolator.

17. *Lo Tonanu*: (Deut. 23:17) 'You shall not taunt him' [the *Ger Toshav*]. This Torah Law mandates cooperation between Jews and *Ger Toshav* in earthly matters, and shows that not only Jews, but also non-Jews have a heritage in Torah Law.

18. *Mekablin*: Forced [*Ger Toshav*] oath, or reason to formally engage with *Ger Toshav*.

19. *Minim*: members of a sect that believes in two or more powers.

20. *Mitzaveh v'oseh*: A higher level (than one who is not commanded) of receiving reward for one's performance of *Mitzvot*. A *Ben Noah* who formally accepts the Seven Laws is considered to be Commanded and Fulfills (*mitzaveh v'oseh*).

21. *Mitzvah l'chiyuto*: A Scriptural *Mitzvah* to support, sustain, and provide for the *Ger Toshav*. Details vary in regard to the intangibles of the 'who, what, why, etc.' of this *Mitzvah* based on the nature of the *Ger Toshav* oath.

22. *Mosrim*: people who turn Jews over to the police or other non-Jewish authorities.

23. *Mumar*: a Jew who spitefully violates the commandments of the Torah.

24. *Nilveh*: literally 'attached': a non-Jew who is no longer identified as a goy [from the nations], becomes a *Ger Toshav*, and goes further to properly attach to Israel, while stopping short of a full-conversion to Israel which would grant Israelite status.

25. *Nochri Chasid*: An elevated gentile, viewed with a good eye because of his love of Israel. Or it can be seen a lesser term of endearment for any one of the various *Ger Toshav* labels that fall short of *Ger Toshav Gamor*, or any sub-category of a righteous gentile/'*Ger Toshav*'/'*Chasid Umot Ha-Olam*'

26. *Notzrim*: Christians.

27. Overcharging: The Torah cautions 46 times to not abuse a '*Ger*'; one of these abuses that is frequently cautioned against, and such that it epitomizes the concept of one Torah for the Native Jew and the *Ger* is the strong prohibition of 'overcharging.'

28. Seven Laws of the Children of Noah: The basic Torah for the non-Jewish nations, consisting of prohibitions concerning idolatry, blasphemy, murder, theft, forbidden

sexual relations, eating the limb taken from a living animal, and failure to establish just courts of law.

29. *Shituf* - literally 'partnership': belief in the God of Israel together with another deity.

30. Three Israelites: A pre-requisite *Bet din* of three observant Jewish men required to grant acceptance of a *Ger Toshav* [among other Torah Law matters that this type of *Bet din* can be used for, apart from that of *Ger Toshav*].

31. *Tzaddik Gamor*: A completely righteous person.

32. *Umot Ha-Olam*: Non-Jews who stand with Israel [nominally, or who at least are not blatantly against Israel] yet who have no allegiance to God or His Torah.

33. Wicked *Acum*: The lowest grade of non-Jew; stands to bring down Israel, God, Torah, etc. This persona carries an agenda to the demise of Israel, God Forbid. The Wicked *Acum* are given the least amount privilege and leniency in Torah Law.

34. *Yisrael Gamor*: A *kosher* Jew either by birth or through conversion.

35. *Zichrono l'Beracha*: 'may he or she be remembered for good,' The term of praise given to the deceased on account of their actions in their lifetime.

36. *Nochri* - literally 'stranger': The Biblical term for what is often used either in slang or from the Talmud to denote a gentile [or *acum*, goy, idolater, etc.]

Lexicon of Terms
Encyclopedic Dictionary For 'Non-Jews in Torah'

(A Guide to Understanding Rabbinic *Noahism Ikkar* Terms and Phrases)

~Advanced Section~

Compiled and written by Rabbi David Katz

Ger: alien, stranger, foreigner [Biblical]; any other definition is Talmudic, i.e. '*Lefi Pshuto*.'

Ger Toshav: legal [fiction] term; a *Ger Toshav* [is a term that] is only defined by its associative '*Ikkar* Term/Phrase.' (Other examples of 'legal fiction' are: Shabbos *goy*, *heter machira*, etc.)

Ger Toshav[102] *'who doesn't serve idols'*[103]: a non-Jew who has turned away from idolatry. A *Ger Toshav* who is associated with the *ikkar* phrase 'doesn't serve idols' generally has a connotation of a proper rejection of idolatry, i.e. has rejected '*shituf*.' (*Shituf* is

---

[102] Legal [fiction] term; see footnote 103.

[103] *Ikkar* phrase... that defines *Ger Toshav* by direct copy and paste from *Avodah Zara 64b*. Many times in the *Chumash* when one will find the word '*ger*,' at first glance in the commentaries it may be listed as *Ger Toshav*. The careful reader will see that this is followed by 'who doesn't serve idols.' Making *ger* into *Ger Toshav* is an example of *Lefi Pshuto*. When we affix 'who doesn't serve idols,' *which is an ikkar* phrase, the *Lefi Pshuto* is expanded, and in this case, it is copied and pasted from *Avodah Zara* 64b. People are often unaware of the Talmudics that are involved as something as simple as *Chumash Rashi*.

any belief in God that attributes shared powers upon the Almighty.) The Jewish commandment from Sinai to reject idolatry implies a rejection of *shituf*. Thus, the non-Jew who rejects *shituf* (with an oath; *kabbalah*) has chosen to perform this commandment (one out of seven of the Noahide Laws) in the way that an Israelite performs the same commandment.

If the non-Jew keeps all Seven Laws of Noah, and rejects *shituf* with an oath in the way that a Jew was commanded to at Sinai, he is not a 'complete *Ger Toshav*' [i.e. a full '*Ger Toshav* in the time of Jubilee'], but rather a 'partial *Ger Toshav*,' or in other words, he is allowed to be called ('in the name of'; 'compared to') *Ger Toshav*. Another term that he may be called is [a 'proper *Ben Noah*'; '*Ben Noah Kosher*'] '*Ben Noah*' – i.e. 'not a complete *Ger Toshav*.'[104]

Ben Noah: Any 'non-Jew.' It can also imply [based on context] one who is attempting to keep the 'Noahide Laws,' or one who is successfully keeping the Noahide Laws. It can also mean one who is not quite a 'full *Ger Toshav*,' i.e. has chosen to take on more than the standard Noahide Law, but 'has not, or cannot, appear before a *Bet din*.' Context will reveal the *ikkar* usage, and provide insight as to connotation.

Ben Noah Kosher: a Ben Noah who has taken on more than the standard Noahide Law. Usually this means a proper rejection of

---

[104] See Rambam, *Hilchot Melachim* 8:10-11; 10:10.

shituf and/or an observance of the '*Ger Toshav Shabbos.*' This term is synonymous with a Proper Ben Noah.

Ger Toshav Shabbos: One who is not a '*Nochri*' by either rejecting *shituf* or 'properly accepting upon one's self the Noahide Laws,' may choose to 'observe the Sabbath' by 'performing *Melacha*,' but refraining from 'performing *Melacha* for a Jew.' This removes the *Ger Toshav* from the category of a '*Shabbos Goy*,' and his Shabbos observance is not considered 'observing the Jewish Shabbos,' for to do so would be considered to 'make a new religion.'

Nochri: a non-Jew, by standing as a non-Israel ideologically. This term is synonymous with *acum*, *goy*, non-Jew, and sometimes *kuti*. *Nochri* is a Biblical term, while the others are Talmudic synonyms.

Ger Toshav who 'properly keeps the Noahide Laws': A non-Jew who formally accepts upon one's self the Seven Laws of Noah. In the times of the Temple this would render one as a complete/full *Ger Toshav*; a proper *Ger* allowed to live in Israel and who is privy to certain rights and advantages. This distinction is given today, albeit on a lower, unofficial level. One can choose to properly accept, and thereby be <u>called</u> a *Ger Toshav*, or one can unofficially accept and be treated like a proper Ben Noah, who is to be considered <u>like</u> a *Ger Toshav*.

Ger 'who eats *neveilah*': The Torah commands that a Jew who comes into possession of *neveilah*, non-*kosher* meat, should either give to a *Ger Toshav* of your gates or sell it to the *nochri*. Biblically the *Ger* is any non-*nochri*. Talmudically, it is *Ger Toshav*, either because he rejects idolatry, or keeps the Seven Laws, or both, or neither; one who minimally doesn't have a religion of idol worship is considered like a *Ger Toshav*. An example of the latter is an Yishmaelite, and the former would be a Noahide – *lefi pshuto*.

Ger Shaar: The Biblical *Ger in your gates*. It does not exist in the Talmud, and it implies a *kosher* non-Jew who is in a working proximity with the Jewish People for the sake of serving God in the *kosher* way. He eats *neveilah*, keeps Shabbos, and listens to the Torah being read at the Temple, as explained by the Bible itself. The Talmud says a *Ger Toshav* can do some of these things as well, but in truth, that would be a *Ger Shaar,* who doubles as a *Ger Toshav,* semantically. The semantics do not always work, and it depends on the *ikkar* and the commentary *lefi pshuto*.

Ger Tzedek: The Talmud uses this term to denote, either a full convert to Judaism, also known as a *Ger Gamor*, or a term used to describe a Canaanite Slave, who is a quasi-convert to Judaism. The Zohar uses this term mystically, or to denote a non-Jew who has overcome many challenges in order to reside spiritually close to Israel/Jews. *Ger Tzedek* is the term used for one who has accepted *mitzvot*.

150

Nilvah: A Prophetic term used to describe a *Ger* (typically non-Jew) who is attached to Israel in a bonded way. The *ikkar* phrase would be '*Nilveh – Ger.*'

Ben Necher: A *nochri* antagonist to Israel.

Ben HaNecher: Someone who has *nochri* ancestry and is uncircumcised either literally, or has no circumcised offspring, *lefi pshuto*. The term implies a longing to attach to Israel despite obvious lacking, and thus is typically grouped with the *Nilveh – Ger*.

Canaanite Slave: A non-Jewish slave who has undergone *mikvah* and *milah*, and has taken on the commandments of a woman. This is not a full convert, but a quasi convert. When we see *Ger Tzedek* in text, it will either be speaking about a full convert or a Canaanite slave. *Ger Tzedek* is called a complete *Yisrael* as opposed to a Native *Yisrael*.

The difference would be that a native *Yisrael* level of conversion can marry a Jew and enters into the third Holy House of Israel, while a full *Yisrael* [conversion] (non-native) chooses to not marry Jewish, thereby remaining in the fourth non-Holy House of Israel. When speaking about a *Ger Tzedek* Canaanite, the Talmud often pairs them with *Ger Tzedek* non-native convert. The native convert is a full Jew, while the *Ger Tzedek* non-native is not a full Jew, but can keep the Shabbos like a Jew. This explanation is *lefi pshuto* and according to rabbinic *ikkar* terms. Often times the *Ger*

Toshav slave and *Ger Tzedek* slave are grouped together, making proper context imperative.

Ger Toshav Slave: A Canaanite slave who does not wish to circumcise or *mikvah*, and only takes on the Seven Laws of Noah, is <u>like</u> a *Ger Toshav*, and is a Canaanite slave.

Ger Toshav Jubilee *Noheg*: A *Ger Toshav* that only exists in the Jubilee year. Typically, this refers to a slave or a runaway slave seeking asylum, or a full Biblical status granting liberty to non-Jews who are working in close capacity with the Jewish People. The righteous non-Jew, through keeping the Seven Noahide Laws, is considered <u>like</u> a *Ger Toshav*, but not the *Ger Toshav* of Jubilee.

Mekablin [Ger Toshav]: A forced acceptance upon someone seeking *Ger Toshav* status for any number of reasons. The coercion also is implied upon a Jew who must comply with Torah should he employ a *Ger Toshav*. Since today we can never be sure if one is a *Ger Toshav*, when Torah penalties are involved or monetary loss could occur, without proper background check or a perfect oath-taking system, the Talmud says, this type of *Ger Toshav* does not exist, accept in a time of Jubilee, and typically in the Land of Israel.

As long as there is no danger or loss that can occur through one being considered *Ger Toshav*, then such a *Ger Toshav* exists at all times and in all places. An example is that the Noahide who rejects *shituf* is considered <u>like</u> a *Ger Toshav*; he does not need the

Jew to remind him to not do *melacha* for the Jew. He himself refrains from doing *melacha* for a Jew, while he does *melacha* for himself. This level of *Ger Toshav*, who observes Shabbos, does not keep Shabbos like a Jew, nor due to a Jewish covenant; his Shabbos observance is a stringent approach to not serving idols, in the same way as a Jew was commanded at Sinai to not serve idols. The Talmud states that to desecrate Shabbos is akin to idolatry. Thus, if the non-Jew performs *melacha* for a Jew, it is akin to idolatry. This *Ger Toshav* has rejected *shituf*, and is considered like a *Ger Toshav*.

Ger Toshav Gamor: A complete *Ger Toshav*, on the level of a *Ger Toshav* at the time of the Temple, or a time of Jubilee. All other *Ger Toshav*, even if called *Ger Toshav*, are not *Gamor*.

'A *Goy* who keeps Shabbos is liable for death': If a *nochri* does not do *melacha* for a Jew because he thinks he is commanded as such, is liable. A *nochri* is not commanded in Shabbos in any way, and only rabbinically is a Jew commanded *lefi pshuto* to remind the *nochri* to not do *melacha* for him. A *nochri* is not a *Ger Toshav*, and the *Ger Toshav* is scripturally reminded to not perform *melacha* for the Jew. The *Ger Toshav* Shabbos is a way to not serve idolatry, and is therefore, categorically not included in the precept against a *goy* who keeps Shabbos.

Lefi Pshuto, a *goy* works 24/7, and thus is defined as a person who does *melacha*. This is a Talmudic *ikkar*. There is never a reason for the *goy* to not do *melacha lefi pshuto*.

'A *goy* who learns Torah is liable for death': The commandment to learn Torah is exclusive for Jews. A Noahide does not have an eighth commandment to Learn Torah [like a Jew]. A Noahide has a commandment of Talmud Torah that is required in order to fulfill the Seven Laws. He gets rewarded as 'one who is commanded and does' when '*dinim*' are performed according to '*Torat Yisrael.*' This is equivalent to a 'personal *kabbalah*,' and this per force makes 'him comparable to a High Priest' and is a display of having 'rejected *shituf.*' [Notice how many *ikkar*im *lefi pshuto* it takes to explain this point; and there are many more one could bring in for comprehension.]

The non-Jew studies Torah wisdom in order to perform a commandment, either for the Seven, or a 'Ben Noah may do any of the commandments according to the *halacha.*' Shabbos and Torah are separate; Shabbos is a part of rejecting idolatry, and Torah we address here.

A Jew who studies Torah, according to the commandment, is not required to perform the law he is studying; his Torah study may or may not be theoretical. The Ben Noah who engages in deep Torah wisdom must apply the wisdom learned by fulfilling the *din*; his study is not Jewish, it is not theoretical. Thus, if he studies like a Jew, out of a desire for the theoretical, he is liable for death [only by the hands of heaven, for he has stolen – *lefi pshuto*, and according to the *ikkar*]. Like all *ikkar*im and *lefi pshuto*, this *ikkar* is merely saying that a Ben Noah may not purely study as a Jew. He may study as a non-Jew, and that means that he may study alone, where acceptable, and/or with a Jew beyond that, even into the theoretical realm. The *ikkar*im are many, as we take into account many factors: is it a *goy*, *acum*, *Noahide*, *nochri*, *Ger*, which kind of *Ger*, etc. Each coordinate will yield revelation to the permission made available to the non-Jew. The death penalty is not literal, it is *lefi pshuto* and refers to stealing. Stealing is one of the Noahide Laws, and thus it is brought here *lefi pshuto*. There are numerous calculations that one can figure of this law. The diligent student will find the *ikkar*im, and work them out *lefi pshuto*; the *Ger* who learns Torah is compared to the *Kohen Gadol*.

'A *goy/acum/nochri/Ger* who learns Torah is like a High Priest': This is a quote from the Talmud, *Baba Kama* 38a. It is often considered non-authoritative folklore/*aggadattah*; it isn't, it is *halachic*. The non-Jew who learns Torah is compared to the High Priest for many reasons; namely because just as a High Priest performs more commandments than a regular Jew, so too, the non-Jew who is involved in Torah in the prescribed way, will find that he has more commandments that he may fulfill, besides the Seven. *B'nai Noah* can bring an offering to the Temple, and can even offer a sacrifice today, while a Jew cannot. The Jew may learn about it in theory, and even aide the non-Jew who receives the theoretical learning from the Jew, and is then able to put theory into practice; the Ben Noah is therefore like a High Priest.

'Commanded and Does': The *B'nai Noah* are commanded to keep Seven Laws, for all time and in every place. Mount Sinai changed history by routing the Seven Laws through the Torah of Moses; Noahide Law must be according to Torah to receive ample reward, as someone who is commanded and does/fulfills. The alternative is to not be commanded, although obligated, and thus the reward is incomplete. The Noahide Laws must be properly accepted onto the Ben Noah with a *kosher kabbalah*/personal acceptance.

Shituf: Attributing another power as God. Roughly, this is any non-*Kosher* belief in God. All organized religion is *shituf*; Noahides are not commanded to reject *shituf*. It is, however, encouraged to reject *shituf* and is praiseworthy. A Jew who identifies a non-Jew who has naturally come to reject *shituf*, has an incumbent obligation to associate with the non-Jew as someone considered to be like a *Ger Toshav*. A *Ger Toshav* does not engage in *shituf*.

Ben Noah - Ger Toshav: A non-Jew must properly accept the Noahide Laws to reclaim the *ikkar* status *lefi pshuto* of 'commanded and fulfills.' This is achieved in *Bet din* and elevates one into a *Ger Toshav*. Ideally, this is the prescriptive route in a time of Jubilee, however, the obligation still exists. A minimal *Bet* *din* of three Jewish Friends may be used to grant a status that is <u>like</u> a *Ger Toshav*; the benefit is to reject *shituf* and to learn Torah and to keep Shabbos *lefi pshuto*. If one cannot appear before *Bet din*, either because it is not a time of Jubilee or if it is too difficult, they may remain a Ben Noah, but are considered as commanded and fulfills. Their status connotes being not a *Ger Toshav Gamor*.

A Commandment to sustain the *Ger Toshav*: The Jew has a Scriptural Commandment to sustain the *Ger Toshav*; the source is the giving of the *neveilah*. Even one who is considered <u>like</u> a *Ger Toshav* is to receive help; the minimal observance of this is that as long as one is not a wicked *acum*, a Jew cannot hurt him, even though he may choose to not actively help him. This is the lowest common denominator, as the appropriate infrastructure to ascertain who is a *Kosher Ger Toshav* will not exist until Jubilee.

Don't taunt the *Ger*: Forty-six times in the Torah we are warned against taunting the *Ger*.

Rabbinic Sources that validate 'Ger' ['Toshav'] B'Zman HaZeh throughout Mesora, Shas, and Poskim

1. *Mishna Breura* 304:3 [see *Biur Halacha*]

2. Ritva to *Makkos* 9a

3. Chofetz Chaim *Sefer HaMitzvot* [#61 Love the *Ger*]

4. Rashi [*Yevamot* 48b and *Devarim* 20:18]

5. Rav Hutner [*Pachad Yitzchak Pesach* 27:2]

6. Rebbe Nachman [*Likutei Moharan Torah* 1:14, 1:17, 2:5:4,5,15]

7. Lubavitcher Rebbe [*Sicha Chelek* 31 *Parashas Mishpatim*]

8. *Shitas* Raavad [*Issurei Biah* 14:7-8]

9. Rav Chaim Kanievsky [*Shulchan Aruch* 304]

10. Rashbah [*Toras Ha-Bayit Beit Hashem*]

11. *Shitas Ha-Meiri* [*Sanhedrin* 59]

12. *Even Ezra* [*Devarim* 27:19 and 31:12]

13. *Makor Sugias* in *Shas* and *Poskim* (*Rishonim* and *Achronim*) [*Yev* 48b, *Krisos* 9a, A.Z. 64b, *Makkos* 9a]

14. Griz on the Rambam [Back of the book; *Ger Toshav*]

15. Rav Kook [concerning *Ger Toshav* and *Shmittah*; *Psak* through his *Bet din*]

16. *Shitas Rogachover Gaon* [*Tzfanas Paneach*; According to 2nd *deah* of *Shitas Ritva*, *Ben Noah* is *Mitzaveh v' Oseh*...]

17. *Tur Shulchan Aruch* [*Yoreh Deah* 117 *Psak* to give *Neveilah* to *Ger Toshav*]

18. *Shulchan Aruch* O.C. 304

19. *Midrash Tanchuma* [*Vaykahal Siman* 8: A *Ger* who learns Torah is like a *Kohen Gadol*]

20. Ramban [*Shemos* 20:10; Commentary to *Chumash*]

21. *Gazeirus HaKasuv Devarim* 14:21 [Commentary Onkelos; *Neveilah* to the *Ger in your Gates*]

22. *Ger Toshav* (*Ger loshon* in *Psukim*) in *Midrash Halacha* [*Sifri*, *Mechilta*, etc.]

23. Rambam *Hilchot Melachim* 8:10-11

24. Rambam *Hilchot Melachim* 10:9-10

25. Rambam *Hilchot Issurei Biah* 14:7-8

26. *Avodah Zara* 64b

27. *Krisos* 9a

28. *Makkos* 9a

29. *Yevamos* 48b

30. Rabbi Ahron Soloveichik's '*Ode Yisrael Yosef Beni Chai*'

31. Rabbi Nevantzhal on *Shavuot* [Ruth the *Ger Toshav*] and *Hilchos Shabbat* [*Krisos* 9a][105]

32. Rabbi Nachum Eliezer Rabinovitch *SHU"T Siach Nachum*

33. *Sefer HaChinuch Mitzvah* #431 [Love the *Ger*]

34. *Piskei Halacha* in *Choshen Mishpat* and *Yoreh Deah* concerning *Ger Toshav* [wine, *lo techanem*, etc.]

---

[105] Rabbi Nevantzhal *paskens* a *Ger Toshav b'zman hazeh* is obligated to keep Shabbos, but absolutely must perform *melacha* that is only forbidden to a Jew, and therefore the *Ger Toshav* does not keep Shabbos like a Jew. The Rav *paskens* like *Krisos* 9a and in accordance to the *Shita* of Rashi. In this case the *Ger Toshav b'zman hazeh* refers to one who is careful in the Seven Laws of Noah and rejects *shituf*; *Mishneh Breura* 304. For more knowledge of *Ger Toshav* and Shabbos see *Likutei Sichas* Vol 31, *Parashas Mishpatim*.

Select Ger Toshav Sources

~~

Excerpts, Adaptations, and unofficial translations by Rabbi David Katz

Shulchan Arukh 304:3

A complete non-Jew who is a hired worker (*sachir*). His *rav* is not commanded concerning his rest [on Shabbos].

Mishna Breura (304:3/24)

'A complete non-Jew...'

...If he accepted upon himself the Seven *Mitzvot*, surely, he is a *Ger Toshav*, and he is forbidden to perform *melacha* [on Shabbos] for a Yisrael, even for one who is not his *rav*, and as we mentioned above.

And look in the Rambam *Hilchot Issurei Biah* 14:7,8 where it says: *'The Law of Jubilee, concerning the Ger Toshav...'* and so an *eved* who does not want to accept upon himself *mitzvot*, except for the Seven *Mitzvot* just <u>like</u> a *Ger Toshav*, also we do not accept him in a time when there is not a functioning Jubilee Year. And the *Ravad* disputes this. Look there.

We see that the *halacha* is like the *Ravad* through the *halachic mesorah* of the *Chofetz Chaim* in the *Mishnah Breura*. Rav Chaim Kanievsky, *shlita*, poskins accordingly today.

Biur Halacha – 'a complete non-Jew'

The Magen Avraham wrote: 'If he accepted upon himself *mitzvot* that are appropriate for a slave, but he is, in fact, a *sachir*, it appears to me that his master is not commanded to make him rest [from *melacha*] that he does for himself. But if he does [*melacha*] for another *Yisrael*, then it is absolutely forbidden from the Torah, i.e., Scripturally, for he is no different from a regular *Ger Toshav*.

HaRav HaGaon Chaim Kanievsky, shlita, Shonei Halachot, Shabbos 304

A *goy* who keeps Shabbos like a Jew is liable for the death penalty and so too a *Ger Toshav*, one who accepted upon himself the Seven *Mitzvot B'nai Noah*, and not to serve Idols, even with *shituf*. There is a difference between a *goy* and a *Ger Toshav*. The *goy* is permitted by the Torah to be commanded to do *melacha* even for a Yisrael and it is only forbidden rabbinically, but the Torah itself forbids a Yisrael to order the *Ger Toshav* to perform prohibited Shabbos labor for him, and he [the *Ger Toshav*] is allowed to do prohibited Shabbos labor only for himself.

In the view of the Rambam, in *Issurei Biah* 14:8, we do not accept *Ger Toshav* except in a time of Jubilee (specifically, a slave who accepts only the Seven Laws which makes him <u>like</u> a *Ger Toshav*). And the *Ravad* argues on this.

Some say as he formally accepts upon himself the Seven Mitzvot [he may also accept] to keep a *Ger Toshav* Shabbos; and also, if he accepted upon himself other mitzvot, then his *status* remains <u>like</u> a *Ger Toshav* in all other matters until he accepts upon himself all other mitzvot as a full convert.

Ritva commentary to Tractate Makkot 9a

There are three categorical terms used for *goyim*: *Ger Toshav, Ben Noah, and goy*. A *Ger Toshav* is one who is received in *Bet Din Yisrael* in order to accept upon himself fulfillment of the Seven Mitzvot that were commanded to *B'nai Noah*. With respect to his acceptance of the Seven Mitzvot in *Bet Din*, he is called one who is '*commanded and fulfills*,' and because of this, we are commanded to support them.

A *Ben Noah* is one who was not received in *Bet Din*, but rather we see that he fulfills the [Seven *Mitzvot*] on his own and receives reward commensurate with one who is '*not commanded but fulfills*,' as it says in *Baba Kama* 38b. And because of this, we are not commanded to support him. However, we must not hurt him or cause him to be executed, for the fact is that he does perform them even though he is not commanded, and therefore receives a partial reward.

Chofetz Chaim Book of Mitzvot, positive mitzvah 61

It is a positive mitzvah to love the *Ger*, for it says: *'And you will love the Ger.'*[106] And this is in addition to the principle *'You will love your neighbor as yourself.'*[107] For, behold, the *Ger* is included in *Klal Yisrael*, and *HaKodesh Baruch Hu* loves the *Ger*. As it is written in *Devarim*10:18, *'Love the Ger to give him bread and garment.'* And it says in *Shemot* 23:9: *'And you all know the nefesh of the Ger.'* The meaning of *'Ger'* here is, *'one who comes from another land and from another city to dwell with us,'* and all the more so, a *Ger* who becomes a *Ger* (*Ger sh'nizgaiyer*). This applies to every place and at all times for both males and females.

Sicha of The Lubavitcher Rebbe Chelek 31 Parashas Mishpatim

The *mitzvah* of *Ger Toshav* is that they themselves are connected to *dinei Yisrael* and *Torat Yisrael*, which is the opposite reason [from being connected to Shabbos] only through their connection to Yisrael. Thus, one who accepts Seven Mitzvot *B'nai Noah* of *Ger Toshav* has a personal affiliation to *Torat Yisrael*, as it was written in Rambam *Hilchot Melachim* 8:10-11.

And how does one accept the Seven *Mitzvot*?

1. He comes before three Jews.

2. This is so because it is written in the Torah of Moshe that [*Ger Toshav*] has an attachment and a personal affiliation

---

[106] *Devarim* 10:19.

[107] *Vayikra* 19:18.

with *Torat Yisrael*. He has accepted upon himself *Torat Yisrael* and lives by the Torah. This means that the Shabbos day is relevant to him and it is not a plain day; it becomes a command for themselves, and it is called *Shabbos Yisrael*.

And here, the *Maggid Mishneh* holds that according to the Rambam, this resting on Shabbos of a slave/servant and *Ger Toshav* is not because of relationship of property or money to Yisrael, but rather because of their affiliation with *dinei* and *Torat Yisrael*. And Rambam says this himself in context of accepting Seven *Mitzvot* of *Ger Toshav*.

And therefore, in matters *specific* to *Yisrael*, when doing *prohibited Shabbos labor for a Yisrael*, it is prohibited under '*commanded Shabbos rest.*' Therefore, the *Maggid Mishneh* explains that the view of the Rambam when speaking about 'a hired worker' means non-specifically, thereby including any non-Jew who keeps the Seven Laws from his own volition, and chooses to attach to Israel and the Torah.

All *prohibited Shabbos labor* for Yisrael is prohibited, and he is called a *Ger Toshav* (or slave since they accepted upon *themselves* Seven *Mitzvot* that were commanded the sons of Noah, and behold, they are <u>like</u> *Ger Toshav*) in that he would be available to perform the prohibited labor had he not been commanded.

However, *acum* who have not accepted the *Seven Mitzvot B'nai Noah,* are not forbidden to do prohibited Shabbos labor for Yisrael, for it is impossible for them to relate to Shabbos. This is the same distinction that we saw in the *Mishna Breura* and in *Shoneh Halachot* above, between the goy and the *Ger Toshav*.

According to the Rogatchover Gaon

The *Ger Toshav* in our time and in the time of the Temple are different, the difference being, whether or not he needs acceptance in *Bet Din*. This is because there is a possibility in our time to influence the Nations of the world to observe the Seven *Mitzvot*. The *Rogatchover* holds that the differences concern the two *halachot* of the Rambam. In *Halacha Issurei Biah* 14:7 he wrote: '*Who is a Ger Toshav...*' this is an *acum* who accepted upon himself not to serve idols and constellations, along with the other laws commanded to the Children of Noah. And in *Hilchot Melachim* 10:10, he wrote, '*B'nai Noah* who want to do the other *mitzvot* of the Torah in order to receive a reward, we do not prevent them from doing it, and they are allowed to do them in accord with the *halacha*.' And he holds that the laws of *Issurei Biah* speak about accepting *gerut* and *bet din*. Therefore, he is considered like a *Ger Toshav*. And in *Hilchot Melachim*, it says that if he did not accept his *gerut* in *Bet Din*, or in a time when the Jubilee Year is not observed, then he is in the category of a *Ben Noah*. That is to say that the view of Rambam has two perspectives:

Ger Toshav who accepts the Seven Laws in *bet din* before three Jews. *Ben Noah* who does not accept them in *bet din* or a time where there is no Jubilee, a time when we do not

168

forcefully receive him, but if he accepts the Seven *Mitzvot* upon himself, we have a commandment to support them.

The differences in simply keeping seven mitzvot *B'nai Noah* and accepting them upon himself as a *gerut* in *Bet Din* is as follows: in the *din* of the *Ger* in his *giur* as a way of keeping the mitzvot, we find two laws in the Rambam, with two different names; in *Hilchot Issurei Biah* 14:7 we obligate *Ger Toshav*, not because he only keeps Seven Laws of Noah, but also because he additionally took it upon himself not to serve idols. And in *Hilchot Melachim*, behold, even though he is called a *Ben Noah*, we can even allow him to keep the rest of the mitzvot of the Torah according to the *halacha*. And the Rogatchover Gaon explained these two distinctions. One who becomes *Ger Toshav* by specifically rejecting idol worship with *kabbalah*, is now warned on *shituf*.

Pachad Yitzhak, HaRav Yitzhak Huttner

...All these things that we have said are only to explain the Seven *Mitzvot*, as to how they were to be kept until the advent of the covenant of 613 mitzvot. Now, at the time of the covenant of 613 *mitzvot* (at Mount Sinai) the Seven *Mitzvot* were renewed, making it possible for *B'nai Noah* to join the covenant of the Seven to the covenant of the 613, and the *Ben Noah* who does this is called a *Ger Toshav*.

And it is clear that the view of Rashi is like the view of those authorities who consider him to be *Ger Toshav* and not a plain *Ben Noah* who keeps the seven mitzvot. Rather he is a renewed *Ger Toshav* that it is possible for him to be a *Ben Noah* who becomes *Ger* for the matter of being obligated on those Seven *Mitzvot* like Israel. Since that with Israel the *halacha* is that a Shabbos desecrator is akin to an *acum*, thus the *Ger Toshav* is obligated on Shabbos from the aspect that he has rejected Idolatry like Israel. And this is a *chidush* (innovative realization) that *Ger Toshav* is obligated on Shabbos from the point of view of the prohibition of Idolatry which we learn in truth from the verse, *Mishpatim* 23:12, according to the view of Rashi. And according to this, Rashi's point of view on *Yebamot* 48b explains *Beitza* 16a, which discusses a non-Jew's relationship to Shabbos.

Avodah Breura[108]

~~

Compliled by Rabbi Yitzchok Mitnick

Unofficial translation by Rabbi David Katz

The Mitzvah to Make Gerim

Question: Is it allowed to go beyond our obligation to make *Acum* into Noahides[109] and bring advanced *B'nai Noah* into a *halachic* reality of having a *'Din Shel Ger Toshav'* [while refraining from entering into a status of *Ger Toshav Gamor*, which is exclusively reserved for a time of Jubilee]? In other words, can we 'Make *Gerim*' when and where appropriate, going beyond our duty of forcefully spreading the Seven Laws of Noah to the Nations?

Tosfos of *Mesechta Avodah Zara* 20a says the following in regards to the need to give the *Neveilah* to the *Ger Toshav* specifically before selling to a *Nochri*: '...(in regards to one's ability to

---

[108] The *Avodah Breura* outlines the full extent a Ben Noah can learn Torah. See *Avodah Breura* compilation to Tractate *Avodah Zara* 2b -3a. Many people think when the Talmud says a goy is liable for the death penalty through either learning Torah or keeping Shabbos, it is literal and dogmatic. The truth of the matter is, concerning learning Torah, a non-Jew who learns Torah is like a High Priest, see the aforementioned *Avodah Breura*. And in terms of Shabbos, see the *psak halacha* of Rabbi Nevantzhal along with the Lubavitcher Rebbe's *Sicha* Vol. 31 and the Brisker Rav who explains how the Patriarchs were able to keep Shabbos before Sinai.

[109] Rambam *Hilchot Melachim* 8:10-11.

misconceive in thinking that we are to convert the *Ger Toshav*) in order that he should take heart and completely convert.' The *Achronim* argue this point, and at the end of this *sugia*, we will arrive to the conclusion that there is a *clear mitzvah* to 'Make *Gerim*.'

...That because it is a *Mitzvah* to make efforts to Make *Gerim*, and behold there is a contrary position in the name of Rabbi Chelbo:[110] '*Gerim* are harsh like overgrowth/skin disease.'

And behold in *Pesachim* 87b is stated: 'Rabbi Elazar says that God only sent Israel into exile among the nations in order to accumulate *Gerim* upon them.' It is implied from this that there is a hint of a *Mitzvah* to make efforts to receive *Gerim* [non-Jewish and convert *Gerim*]. And thus, Abraham our Father made efforts in this as did King Shlomo, according to *Yalkut Shimoni*. King Shlomo loved women from the *goyim*, in order to make them into *Gerim* and to bring them under the wings of the *Shechinah*.

And the *Chasam Sofer* wrote that Rabbi Yehuda held that there is a *Mitzvah* to Make *Gerim*.

And behold there is a way to explain the distinction of *Ger Toshav* in two different ways:

---

[110] *Yevamos* 47b.

a) A Complete *Ben Noah*, only concerning known *Dinim* is his *Din* equal to Israel, because he is from the *Chasidei Umot HaOlam* as it is written by the Rambam.

b) He is categorically removed from being classified as a *Ben Noah*, and even though that he has not entered into *K'lal Yisrael*.

And this is similar to the slave. Were it not for the revelation of the *pussuk* that obligates them into the *Mitzvot* like a woman, he would be exempt from everything, because even though he already left the distinction of *Ben Noah,* he still hasn't entered into *K'lal Yisrael*. And thus, we see from the Language of Rabbeinu Gershom,[111] who wrote that *Ger Toshav* is a matter of '*Ktzat Geirus*.'

And thus, we see from the Language of the Rashba concerning the *Ger Toshav*: 'That a *Ger* who becomes *Ger* is like a newborn child.' Behold, that this principle of a '*Ger* who becomes *Ger* is like a newborn child' also refers to [becoming] a *Ger Toshav*. And this can only be understood if we say that he is removed from being a *Ben Noah*. And thus, we see from the Language of the *Taz* who wrote that a *Ger Toshav* – is one who is categorically removed from being considered belonging to the nations.

And if we say that he is already removed from the category of *Ben Noah* then there is no difficulty, that only concerning a *Ben Noah* is

---

[111] *Krisos* 9a.

there no *Mitzvah* to 'Make him into a *Ger'* for '*Gerim* are harsh on Israel like overgrowth/skin disease,' but for one who has already left the category of *Ben Noah* and only hasn't entered into *K'lal Yisrael*, the *Mitzvah* to 'make them into *Gerim'* is appropriate.

Conclusion: We see that there is a unanimous agreement from the *Poskim* that *Ger Toshav* is a *Mitzvah* that one can engage in today. The Wisdom of how to do so is clear, as well. We are to spread the Seven Laws of Noah[112] and should any *B'nai Noah* find themselves in a new territory beyond the category of *Ben Noah* [from having fully left idolatry, rejecting *Shituf*, and fully keeping the Seven Laws, all under personal acceptance with the proper intention of having been commanded by the Torah of Moses directed at the God of Israel] then it is a *Mitzvah* to Make *Gerim* and the fear of '*Gerim* are harsh onto Israel...' no longer applies. Such a person would have effectively become a self-made *Ger Toshav*, and a Jew would then be able to do a *Mitzvah* of Making *Gerim*. This is called a partial conversion, and the Rashba states that all language of 'A *Ger* who becomes *Ger'* (a *Ger sh'mis'gayeir*) applies to both the full conversion [*Ger Tzedek*] and to a partial conversion [*Ger Toshav*].

In short, we are commanded to emulate Abraham our Father, where appropriate in mainstream *halacha*, as evidenced by a unanimous view among all Torah Sages. The only dispute that takes place is when a source speaks of either a *Ben Noah* or a *Ger*

---

[112] Rambam ibid.

Toshav. The consensus view is that a *Ben Noah* should not be encouraged directly into a status of *Ger Toshav*, while a self-made *Ger Toshav* may be subject to a *halachic* action of Making *Gerim* according to the *halacha*. For this the Torah has warned us forty-six times to not taunt the *Ger* and to make sure to Love the *Ger*.

The Brisker Rav (here, on facing page) and The Lubavitcher Rebbe (*Likutei Sichos* Vol. 31 *Parashas Mishpatim* and *Shaarei Halacha v'Minhag*) together comprise and express the accepted *shita* of the *Ger Toshav* of today (non-Yovel) in *Halacha*, based on Rambam *Hilchot Melachim* 8:10-11. The greater *Ger Toshav Sugia* (how it works and how it is applied for our times) comes to full light through the later works of Rabbi Ahron Soloveichik and Rabbi Nachum Eliezer Rabinovitch.

הילפוותא מערב ועבד כנעני, דגם כשכחר מקבל לא אחר נותן
מקרי כסף תמים, וכמו לדעת שחר הראשונים, ואין חילוק
כלל בין הרמב"ם והרלב"ם בענין כחשם של ע"ע
ועבד כנעני.

מה שכתבת למלק בענין הפיוסא קודושין בין חייבי כריתות
גחייכי נלאוין, לענו נראה בעני המחלוקת כזה, רק בכולים
הא דלא תפסי קודושין משום האישור הוא, ומ"ל שוין לחייבי
כריתות כזה, ואין לחלק בינייהו, אולם מה שכתבת בסוף
דבריך דגם לפי הטעם דאין עשה דוחה ל"ת שש בו כרת
מ"מ הא דנפקענא הזיקק לגמרי הוא רק מעטעמא דלא תפסי
בה קדושין, ובכאחא כן מדברי הרמב"ם בפ"א מהל' יבום
עיי"ש, דבריך נלאון בזה לפום ריהטא כי רחון אנכי מתה
מהשגין, וכמו אשר אמרת, אולם בעיקר הקושיא מנדה לא
בועלה בזה כלום, כי הגם כי' הוא רק לענין הפקעת הזיקה
וכן כם דברי הרמב"ם אמנרים רק לענין הפקעת הזיקה חב
הוא כתובו בחאישם קודושין, דוק בלשוו, אבל לענין פיקד
מלוות יבום הגם לא קיי"ל דגם בח"ל אם בעלו לא קנו אם אף
לית בכו דין דח"י כמבואר בסינ"ולא דף ו' דקמחיב מכן דלם
בעלו קנו, וכן פסק גם הרמב"ם בפ"א כרלב"ל דבמלמדה מן
הנשאין אם בעלו לא קנו משום דאין בעמה דוחה ל"ת מפטם
וגבי נדה הרי קני ועבר מלוה ולטל שש גריעותא בהייבום
שלה, ובשני' דנדה שאני בעולה דינא משאר עריות ומ"ל, שאין
איסורה שיק בכלל לענין שיק דין יבום, רק דמשובה כביאה
בשעתה אשורה ומל"א ני נקרית או המלוה, אבל אין איסורה
שורה בכלל לעיקר דין היבום, ומחמ"ש גם בנדה"ל דקעכעד
על האישור מ"ח לענין מלוות יבום אין זה נוגע כלום וקני
ומקיים מלוה, אבל בשאר חייל אם דאיפשו בכו קודושין אבל
מ"מ איפשורן שוחר למלוה ויבום, ומחמ"ש אם לריכוי בכן
לדין דח"י אבל בלא דח"י אם דהזיקה לא נפקעת מ"מ לא קנה
קנין גמור ואין בויחתה פוערת לרחם ובמבואר בסנ"ולד.
ולמחמא כן, דעטעמא דכך מלמחא לריך פירש וביחא דלית
בחמת חלוקה נזה משם על ונדה מ"ח רק דתפסו בם קודושין,
רק גם בטריקה איסורו ועלה החאפילא שלה לא דמי' לשאר
עריות מ"ח, דאין איסורם שיק בכל לכלומין ובשחן שחחשב
אשר שאימורה על ישמא, רק ממעש הביאה בשעתה אסורה,
ובמכותבר גרמזכ' פריה מהל' יחום דביאו דמ"ם ולא נעשה
זומב מטום ואינך בכלל מלום אשר שאתמורה להעמא לא, מטאש"
כשאר עריות ומ"ל כמבואר בדברי הרמב"ם שם, וכיון דליוטורה
מ"ם פערוא בכבואה לגד חין אם חטיורה כלל לעיקר דין יבום.
אבל בכנ"ש אין שיו"ר, אם מפורש בדברחל דבחמ"ל ועלה אם
דתפסי בכו קודושין אבל מ"ח איסורן שוחר בענין חתפלא
למלוה ויבום ואם בעלו לא קני, ורק משום דין דח"י הוא
דקיימ"ל בכו מלוה יבום בשלמות, ובגדה בעלה בחחפלא אין
כאן פטורא כלל, וכן כן דברי כתום', ומעחיה ל"ם שיך בה
מענחא דרכ של כלל, כיון ואין אחן לריכין כם לדין דח"י כלל
רק המלוה מחקיימת גם בנדתה ואיטוהה, ולקמ"ט.

מש"כ כזדר"נ בענין גר תושב דלא דמיא קבלתו לגיודת של
גר לדק שעתבם ערי ישראל ונתחייב במלות אבל
בכאל הרי גם קודם קבלה מחויב הוא כד מלות ועבר הוא
לאחר קבלה כמו קודם קבלה, בודלאי הדבר כן הוא דלענין
חייב מלות לא נתחדש מ"י קבלתו שום דבר, ולא נחוסופו
עליו שום חיובים על כל בנ"נ דעולמא. אבל מה שהוסים ל"רב

עוד ,,דבמלואא שכל דיני גר חושב אינו אלא כיום לישיבחו
בוניגו בארך", ז"א שבנוגע לגבר חושב בעלמו לא נחחדש ע"י
קבלתו דבר וכל עולמו ומהותו של גר חושב כמו חופב הוא
לושראל כמו להותיבו בארך ובדווטה, וע"י הוא דלמאר כו
דין דאין גר חושב ניהב אלא זמן שהיוב־ל ניהג, ע"י חחמו
אני, דהלא הרבה דינים יש שחון נהב נהם שום שויוהה לישראל
והם נהובנים רק בנניה כלגד ולא בבניה, רב"ג שהרב בשוגג
נכרב ובניה גולה, וכן לעבין הרב דקנאים פוניעין בו מבואר
ברמב"ם דאינו ניהב בבניה, ועוד רבות כאלה, הרי דהקבלה
שנעשה על ידי גביה חדשה דינים גם לענין הגניה בעלמו,
דכהחורה חלקה כין בניה לב"ב, ואמנם כן דלם יחזר מקבלתו
בודאי וכי דינו כביש דעלמא, דבניבו לא נתחוב דבר רק
שכל בשבדו קבלתו, אבל כל זמן שהוא עומד בקבלתו הרי
החיוב מחמ לו דינים וחלקם בינו ובין ב"כ סחתמא. ולפי"ז
גם כך דייל דאין דין ב"ח ניהב אלא בזמן שהיוב־ל ניהב כמ־שר ב"י, דלמ
ברמב"ם שיכר הדין הוא דבשמם שאין היוב־ל ניהב מין
מקבלין, וממילא דה"ה כב"ש פשוט כן בדעת הרמב"ם, אולם דעת
בואה שכחב נ"ב פשוט הין כן בדעת הרמב"ם, אולם דעת
הרלב"יד אחרת נדק לענין דינים מיוחדים הוא דחלוי
זמן שהיוב־ל ניהב, אבל שעת הרמב"ם כמעב פשוטה ומפורשת
כ"י.

והנה כמ־בריי מדבריי ידידי דוקפאר לו כל עיקר כך מילחא
דקנלא זו מה הוא, כיון רבכר מחיוב ועומד הוא
נזה, אולם נראה שאין זה קשה כלל, דהרי בדברי הרמב"ם
מבואר דנעשה משם מפי הגבורה ובשורל לכוב את כל ב"ל עולם
לקבל עליהם שבע מלות שנלטוו ב"נ ואם לא יקבל יהרב, הרי
דלאעיד דבי' מלות עוד נלטוו מיחמ אד"סי ז, אבל לאחר
מ"נ נתחדש דין גם אלל אוה"ע שלא די בזה שאינו עוברני
על ד שי מלות רק לריכים קבל ואם לאו יהרב, וזה דין
שנתחדש על אוה"ע בעמלמם משעת מ"ח ואינד, וגם בכל ד"וא
שם לעבין זה שחוהירו אלה"ע יא לכן חלק לשוי"א כתב כך
דהקבל שבע מלות וחובה, הרי דלא ד' נזה שמהר
לשמותם רק לריך קבל ואם אמי לשמותם כלא הקבלה אינו
בכלל חסידו אוה"ע, וגם הקבלה לריכה לכיות שיקנים אותן
הרמב"ם שם, שכל זה דברים המחדשם שנתחדשו משעת מיח
ואילך אד' גל מלות הוא נ־לאד בירמב"ד מכות דף עי בכתב
חיל גר חושב הוא מקבל ב"ע וכ גבי שקבל כב"ד מלות אלי
מלוה ושובע ערי' ורה"ר יב־ע קבל כב"ד אבל דקים לן
שמקיום אוחן מעלמן הוא ב"ה נדון בהם כמי שאינו מלוהו
ועשם מדמחוב עמד ויומד ארך רלב־ז כם־ש עבד מכדיאל
כביע על עב"ל הרי לשוריכן קבלה על זה
מלות שנלטוו עליהם הוא מדויום שנחחדשו בשעת מיח והוא
נכל כך דלא ריהר כן דברי הרמב"ן כביעל דף ל"ח דעמד
שמקיום לכם שיחבבו כאת מלוי ופושם ומ־ה הוא ישוד
דין דלריכין קבל עליהב, וכ"ב ברמב"ן שם, וכיע כמעיא,
דברי הרמב"ם בכל מלבם שבכ־ה הדר־נ שפתם אלא יכר
כישראל לכל דבר או יכרב, חמורים מאד מאד, דהרי
החם כבר הוא ישראל גמור אל דיניו, ומה בינו לשאר ישראל,
ואם ר"ל שנהחחיב מחך בשבל אוחה דבר מחי קמי"ל דאחר
דין נאמד בזה, סוף דבר דברי הרמב"ם חמורים מאד ואין
לכם שום מקום לבחורה.

Chidushei Maran Riz HaLevi on the Rambam, in the back of the book, section on Ger Toshav

177

Made in the USA
Middletown, DE
26 March 2023

27689338R00099